7-4

Penguin Education

The Myth of Cultural Deprivation

Edited with an Introduction by Nell Keddie

The Myth of
Cultural Deprivation

Edited with an Introduction by Nell Keddie

Penguin Education

Penguin Education
A Division of Penguin Books Ltd,
Harmondsworth, Middlesex, England
Penguin Books Inc, 7110 Ambassador Road,
Baltimore, Md 21207, USA
Penguin Books Australia Ltd,
Ringwood, Victoria, Australia

First published 1973
This selection copyright © Nell Keddie, 1973
Introduction copyright © Nell Keddie, 1973

Made and printed in Great Britain by
Cox & Wyman Ltd,
London, Reading and Fakenham
Set in Intertype Lectura

Contents

Introduction[1]

The papers in this collection have been brought together to raise problems about the appropriateness and consequences of the concept of cultural deprivation. One of its pervasive uses has been as an explanation of failure at school among children of various ethnic and social-class groups and it is possible that the institutionalization of the concept has increasingly put these children at a disadvantage in terms of what is expected from them from the day they enter school. In raising questions about the nature of the concept and its use, we must inevitably raise wider issues about education – curriculum reform and deschooling – and ultimately about what we take to be the prevailing values in the society in which we live.

We can locate the context of the concept of cultural deprivation in the manner in which educational research has been carried out, with its focus on the child rather than on the whole educational situation in which he plays a part. Commonly the child is conceived of as an object with attributes that can be measured, so that the focus has been on creating, for example, objective measures of ability, rather than on interactional contexts and on teachers' ways of assessing and typifying students and on the ways in which teachers and students interpret and give meaning to educational situations.

Researchers in education, seeking the neutrality and objectivity of scientific inquiry, have most commonly treated the child as an a-social object (rather than subject to himself and others) whose attributes can be measured by a battery of tests to reveal his intelligence quotient, social adjustment, achievement motivation, etc. While it is generally admitted that IQ tests cannot be culture-free, the main thrust of the research on educational achievement since the 1950s has been to attempt to explain why children from the poorer groups in our society fail to do as well at school as measures of their intelligence suggest they should. The way the problem is conceptualized

1. I should like to thank Michael F. D. Young of the University of London Institute of Education for his critical reading of this introduction, together with many helpful suggestions.

determines of course the kind of hypotheses, research methodology and findings that feature as explanations of educational failure and success.

As everyone knows, including teachers who learn it in college or, as Estelle Fuchs's paper suggests, on the job, social class and ethnic origin feature both as common-sense and as social science explanations of the rates of educational achievement. A popular and influential study carried out in this tradition in Britain was J. W. B. Douglas's *Home and School* (1964).

The term cultural deprivation became popular in the 1960s among educationalists, especially psychologists, to refer to the complex of variables it was believed were responsible for retarding the child's progress in school. It is well worth examining the assumptions underpinning the term since they reveal the difficulties that must inhere in any attempt to carry out research that claims to be value-free. In the first place it is not clear of what culture these families and their children can be deprived, since no group can be deprived of its own culture. It appears therefore that the term becomes a euphemism for saying that working-class and ethnic groups have cultures which are at least dissonant with, if not inferior to, the 'mainstream' culture of the society at large. Culturally deprived children, then, come from homes where mainstream values do not prevail and are therefore less 'educable' than other children. The argument is that the school's function is to transmit the mainstream values of the society and the failure of children to acquire these values lies in their lack of educability. Thus their failure in school is located in the home, in the pre-school environment, and not within the nature and social organization of the school which 'processes' the children into achievement rates. This individualization of failure – the perception of the problem as one in which teachers are faced with the difficulties presented by individual children – rests on a concept of mainstream culture that is by definition, in the use of indices such as income, occupation, education, etc., a minority culture: the culture of the middle class, which is then said to stand for 'society at large'. It is not the question whether middle-class culture (whatever that vague term means) is desirable or not, nor which of its values deserve to be transmitted to the next generation, but rather the recognition that mainstream and middle-class values are one and the same thing and that neutrality in the construction of indices is impossible. The papers brought together here make this point and in doing so raise questions rather than provide answers. More explicitly they illustrate how concepts of education like notions of who is 'educable' are socially constructed.

Recently research has concentrated on attempting to show that the crucial feature of cultural deprivation is linguistic and cognitive deprivation; this makes Labov's work of very timely relevance since he raises a whole complex of questions about the socially constructed nature of language, education, ability, etc. In the specific area of language he shows that standard English, as the term implies, is taken to be the language of the mainstream culture and, as he and Torrey show, the nonstandard forms of the language which the children speak in their home environments is discouraged in school and thought by both teachers and researchers to be inadequate as a vehicle for logical or formal thought. His argument and data suggest, however, that speakers of nonstandard English are not necessarily without the linguistic and cognitive experience capable of performing the intellectual tasks set by the school: black English (and by implication working-class English, since there is no work drawing on actual speech to suggest the contrary) is capable of sophisticated argument, logic and conceptualization. That is, Labov treats the speech of these children as a dialect and not different in kind from the forms of speech needed to express abstract thought.

If Labov *is* right it becomes interesting to ask why so different a view has prevailed, and why it is that with the children before their eyes teachers and researchers have failed to see what kids from poor homes are capable of. Doubtless the assumption that middle-class culture is the mainstream and necessary culture of the society at large has had much to do with this, for it seems to account for the ignorance of the middle classes about other groups' ways of life which leads them to see the possibilities of ways of life different from their own in a negative light. To refer again to the paper by Fuchs: it is possible that teachers (and why not researchers too?) learn this perception on the job; it is a way of seeing that they 'catch' from the older teachers around them, although the experience of these teachers does not necessarily, as the young teacher will tend to feel, make their perception 'correct'. There are some studies which suggest that many black kids are bicultural and bilingual, experienced participants in more than one culture – an accomplishment they 'hold over' the middle class. It is possible that Larry, could he ever be bothered to do so, could have translated his own speech into standard English. The fact that Labov feels he needs to make this 'translation' illustrates very clearly the kind of difficulty we are speaking of since he seeks to make Larry acceptable to us, not on Larry's terms, but by showing us that Larry's speech can be shown to conform to the strictest principles of Aristotelian syllogisms. The difficulty illustrates how *logics are socially constructed* and are socially situated among the group to whom they are *the* logical way of thinking and doing. (We shall return to this point later since I want to argue that the formal logic of Western culture is no different in this respect from the logic of any other social group and that this has far-reaching implications for what is accounted appropriate school knowledge.) One practical outcome of a serious reading of Labov's work might be a redirection of educational research away from attempting to formulate how to make children more like teachers. It would be more sensible to consider how to make teachers more bicultural, more like the children they teach, so that they can understand forms of English which they do not themselves use as native speakers.

By the standards of most social science research in education, where the methodology has led to the subject being treated as object in the interests of standardization by measurement and quantification of supposedly common attributes, Labov's work has no place at all. He has indices for measuring the attributes neither of speech nor of children, and his sample is, of course, pitifully small. But, as Labov argues, this is to miss the point that human beings actively give meaning to situations and that these meanings are not invariable since they are contexted and embedded in social interaction. He demonstrates not only that researchers often use highly dubious indices to decide what counts as linguistic competence, but also that by ignoring the social context in which the research is undertaken they fail to see that their findings are an artefact (and not merely a variable) of the research situation. Both Labov and Torrey suggest that those 'findings' which are taken to demonstrate the deficiency of these children and to be explicable in terms of factors antecedent to the school or test situation may instead be a situational product of the way in which the children cope with both school and test situations, together with the way in which teachers and researchers interpret the children's response.

Labov is arguing that black Harlem children are not deficient but are already experienced participants in a way of life. Those who argue the deficit theory (see, for example, the Report of the Plowden Committee) point out that the children come from poor homes, often slums, live in overcrowded conditions which deny access to privacy, and lack variety in their surroundings which leads to stimulus-deprivation resulting in cognitive deficiencies and a poor attitude to learning. It is argued that these children lack pre-school educational experiences: books, educational toys and proper parental guidance and interest. The result is said to be that 'normal development' is inhibited and the child's maturational ceiling is lowered. His concentration and memory are said to be poor and his perceptions underdeveloped partly because of the lack of organization of both space and time in the home, which thus fails to provide a structured environment for the child and few possibilities of learning to discriminate and categorize.

It has been pointed out by Baratz and Baratz (1970) that the indices used to measure degrees of structure in the home tend to be drawn from such things as middle-class mealtime schedules and that there has been almost no fieldwork in the area, most of the data being collected by questionaire or interview methods in conditions alien to the respondents. This kind of research and its findings have been termed by Wax and Wax (1964) a 'vacuum ideology', which involves teachers and administrators seeing the problem as one in which individual children present problems because they lack experiences supposedly needed to make them educable, rather than seeing them as children who are already experienced participants in a way of life, albeit one different from their own.

Wax and Wax studied children's experiences in Indian reservation schools. Here one of the educational administrators explains to the Waxes the 'problems' of educating the Sioux Indian child. His explanation seems to rest on the notion that education for these children is like filling empty vessels and it is compounded with almost total ignorance of the Sioux way of life:

The school got this child from a conservative home, brought up speaking the Indian language and all he knows is grandma. His home has no books, no magazines, radio, television, newspapers: it's empty! He comes into school and we have to teach him everything . . . The Indian child has such a *meagre* experience. When he encounters words like 'elevator' or 'escalator' in his reading he has no idea what they mean. But it's not just concepts like these. Take even the idea of *water*. When you and I think of it, well, I think of a shining stainless steel faucet in a sink running clean and pure and of the plumbing that brings it, and chlorination and water purification, or of the half-million-dollar project for the Pine Ridge water supply. But the Indian child doesn't think of water as something running into a bath tub.

Wax and Wax speak of the Sioux traditions of folklore and of the stories that Indian children hear, but comment that many white educators believed that these children 'have no experience in art or music' and argued that 'we must go back to the (Indian) home to find the lack of patterns that should have been learned'.

There is a danger here of seeming to romanticize the poverty of the Indian homestead, but Wax and Wax usefully point to the danger of assuming that those who lack material benefits are necessarily deficient in their culture. What most deserves comment here is that the 'vacuum ideology' pervades descriptions of children from quite different cultures, so that the pictures in the literature of the British working-class child, children on the Indian reservations or poor blacks are strikingly similar. Teachers, administrators and researchers tend to see the features of a way of life different from their own in a negative light. This 'vacuum ideology' or deprivation theory is illustrated, as Labov and Gladwin show, by the frequent failure of these children to perceive and discriminate in ways in which the tests are designed to measure. This failure is not only because of the meanings these tests have in the social context in which they are administered, but also because it seems that patterns of thought, logic and perception have to be learnt rather than treated as the normal development of intelligence in any child. These papers, especially those by Labov and Gladwin, are important because they suggest that so-called minority-group cultures may be seen as not only adequate in their own right, but perfectly competent to conceptualize logically and imaginatively. The perception of these cultures as deficient seems to arise from the ignorance of those who belong to what they perceive as the dominant cultural tradition. It is significant that there is very little research to draw on at the moment to substantiate this view. There are almost no eth-nographies of classroom life in Britain and no extended study of the actual speech of children (working- or middle-class) in interactional learning situations. There are now some studies from the United States, a fact which is probably a reflection of the political situation of blacks and their increasing insistence on the value of their own culture.

It is important to situate or context these studies carried out in the States to weigh both the creative importance and the limitations of a paper such as Labov's. It can be argued that since the typifications of so-called culturally deprived groups are so similar and seem to be the construction of an outgroup, we in Britain should reconsider the notion that working-class speech is unable to cope with what are felt to be high-level abstractions and consider whether, like black nonstandard English, it is better seen as a dia-lectical variation of standard English rather than a different kind of speech from that required for formal and logical thinking. We have no means of knowing at the moment how generalizable argu-ments like Labov's might be, and our ignorance in the British con-text may well reflect a different socio-political situation from the racist conflict in the States. What is clear is that interactional studies like Labov's, which insist on the interactional ongoing qual-ity of speech and the situated nature of meanings, cannot be reduced to positivistic quantitative validation. Whatever direction the at-tempts to sophisticate the analysis take, it is bound to fail to take account of the socially situated and constructed meanings of speech, particularly if validation is believed to reside in the need to ascribe invariant meanings to quantifiable indices. This means, in effect, that positivism – the attempt of the social sciences to emulate the neutrality and so-called objectivity of the natural sciences – cannot tell us what is interesting to know about language: its situated elus-ive complex of meanings.

If attempts like Labov's to focus on the socially contexted mean-ings of speech for participants are taken seriously, then the consequences for researchers and for practical implementation in educational situations are manifold, complex and necessarily uncertain; there are certainly no quick or easy answers to the questions raised for educational practice. Here we may centre on a focal issue that may very generally be located as the socially constructed and situated nature of knowledge.

The issue is most broadly raised in Margaret Mead's paper and allows us to reflect on the precarious nature of what counts as knowledge in various social situations. We tend to take for granted the division between vocational and liberal education and much educational debate focuses on what should appear on the curriculum for whom. For example, the notion of 'relevance'; why are 'Newsom children' supposed to need 'relevance'? Or, equally interesting, why is 'relevance' comparatively irrelevant for 'academic' students? What do we know about students' notions of relevance, and what are the implications of relevance for social control – some lingering desire to 'gentle the masses'? The taken-for-granted assumptions that we can or should distinguish between liberal and vocational education and between school and nonschool knowledge are contexted and not necessary divisions as we conceive them. If we look at 'developing' and at some socialist countries we find that such divisions, as we conceive of them, have not been set up. For example, in North Korea and China students in school undertake agricultural and other productive work as part of their education which does not therefore become only a preparation for adult life. It is relevant and salutary to remember here that 'childhood' and 'adolescence' have their relevance as socially constructed categories and not biological givens in so far as their social location and meaning vary enormously across cultures.

Mead's paper can lead us to see as problematic the definitions of knowledge that are institutionalized or reified (their 'out-thereness' to be mastered rather than experienced) in our school curricula and their relation to what is counted as nonschool or common-sense experiential knowledge. Mead notes that

Just as the presence of proselytizing religion focuses attention upon the means of spreading truth, upon pedagogy, so the implications of social stratification focus attention upon the content of education and lay the groundwork for an articulate interest in the curriculum.

We may take the analogy between religion and education seriously for Mead is suggesting the manner in which 'the idea of Truth, as the revelation of some one group' is spread to or imposed on others. This is an aspect of power as related to the social distribution of knowledge which has been little explored, since the problem has usually been conceptualized in terms of social structure and differentiation as determinants of social stratification. It is linked to the notion of a 'vacuum ideology' since, as Torrey points out, many children come to school to find their experience disvalued and discounted: they are treated as empty, to be filled with knowledge, rather than as experienced participants in a way of life that has its own validity. Torrey is one of the few who argue (though the rise of Afro-American college courses suggests her point is gaining more force) that black culture should become part of school knowledge. More frequent is the 'bridging' concept: that 'minority' cultures should be respected to the degree that they can be used to get the children into the mainstream culture the school is concerned to transmit. That is, most children's experience and many people's way of life is to be seen as inadequate and of limited value. The justification for this lies in the cultural-deprivation thesis: that these cultures are unable to provide members with the conceptual tools for comprehending the 'bodies' or 'forms' of knowledge which have historically come to count as school knowledge.

This view of knowledge, of how to be intelligent in school, sees the curriculum, in the words of Maxine Greene (1971), 'as a structure of socially prescribed knowledge . . . external to the knower, there to be mastered, learned' rather than 'a possibility for him (the learner) as an existing person, mainly concerned with making sense of his life-world'. In what are called 'simple societies', such as those Mead, Frake and Gladwin write about, it is to be assumed that this problem of mastering knowledge not obviously concerned with the learner's life-world arises less frequently. It is indeed one of Mead's central points that where knowledge is not reified and externalized as an 'out-there' facticity, the emphasis in education must be on the wish to learn rather than on the desire to teach.

What Postman's polemic raises for consideration is the possibility that school knowledge in our society need not be so hived off (as academic knowledge usually is) from the life-worlds, present and future, of learners, and not, in that respect, so different in our 'complex society' from the knowledge that becomes available in the education of young people in small-scale societies. In asking what reading is for, what literacy is about, Postman argues that school education as it is practised must be a form of social control with political implications (using both the narrower and wider meanings of power and coercion). This, together with his suggestions of how the mass media might become an integral, natural and meaningful part of school education, is the paper's strength. Not only is it clear that school education is historically and technologically stagnant but that the insistence on literacy is peculiar to school education and not to the life-worlds of learners (who would here include teachers) in most other contexts of their social lives. These are increasingly permeated by other media, as well of course as by talk, which stands as *the* permanent permeating medium of communication but which is frequently treated as irrelevant for the assessment of students in school whose primary tool has to be literacy.

The weakness of Postman's paper is it's post-McLuhan naïvety in the assumption that because the media of learning might be changed the power relationships and the nature of assessment would therefore undergo radical change. How that could happen within the context of schooling (as opposed perhaps to deschooling) as we know it, it is impossible to say, since schools currently play so prominent a role in the assessment and certification of future citizens. It is far from clear why the ability to be literate in terms of standard English should *of necessity* indicate an appropriate occupational niche. However, within the given assumptions of mainstream or middle-class culture, there is no problem in accounting for the school's function in allocating students to the occupational system, as is made clear when one considers such accounts as Olive Banks's (1971) in the widely-read *The Sociology of Education*.

What Postman's paper lacks, to carry the conviction he pleads, is the recognition that 'logics' are socially situated, and that it is because they are so situated and contexted that they must be meaningful if they are ever to become part of the life-world of the learner. The reified curriculum is conceived of only as historically located, the outcome of a number of historical occasions in which what is relevant knowledge has evolved and been incorporated into the 'curriculum'.

We can see in the papers of Labov and Fuchs how conceptions of the learner, the pupil, are socially constructed, located and acquired; Gladwin and Frake can help us to understand, or at least try to conceptualize, by implication and extension of their arguments, how 'logics' may also be so constructed, located and acquired. Mead's point is that one group may impose its logic or 'truth' on another and that this is a form of colonization, be it the 'truth' a missionary imposes on darkest Africa or a middle-class white on an Indian-reservation, black-Harlem or lower working-class child. The assumption in the West, is that formal logic is absolute rather than relative or socially situated (culture-bound), 'abstract' rather than 'concrete' and that historically realized forms of knowledge operate with particular rules and procedures in an unproblematic (insofar as the application of the rule is not generally seen as problematic) way. The legitimating power of this so-called formal logic we have already observed in Labov's transformation of Larry's speech into the formal syllogisms of Aristotelian logic. This problem of how we come to understand logics not our own is also apparent in the ways in which Frake and Gladwin understand their data and seek to make it available to us.

Both Frake and Gladwin provide good grounds for supposing that Western formal logic is not absolute but, like other logics, culture-bound or socially situated, and that certainly the learning of any 'logic' is a highly situated activity which cannot be treated as though it were context-free if it is to become part of the life-world of the learner and to be understood by him at all. Frake raises the very important question of what counts as intelligent behaviour in a particular social context. Gladwin makes it clear that our conception of intelligence in education is intelligence as measured by IQ tests. We have, after reading his paper, to ask not only whether navigating a boat is not like driving a car, but whether either is really qualitatively different from doing a sum or reading a book. All activities are marked by the relation betwen theoretic and practical operations which are more familiarly distinguished as 'abstract' and 'concrete'. (This is a point to which we shall return since the contention is that Gladwin demonstrates just how setting up a distinction between the two creates problems to be solved which need not be differentiated as problems in the first place.) We should have to ask, for instance, whether a Western navigator could 'gloss' the rules in use.

What might concern us about learning in school is how knowledge is made available and how children are expected to, and set about trying to, acquire the rules for knowledge in use. In Frake's terms: how do children discover the procedures for 'determining the rules of use', in what are too often assumed to be presented as context-free abstractions: 'a structure of socially prescribed knowledge, external to the knower, there to be mastered', to quote Maxine Greene's words again.

Frake's paper, which might at first reading seem to have little to do with school experiences, can be read as very apposite to those experiences. Frake the anthropologist has to learn not only the substantive vocabulary of medicine, but also its 'rules in use' which arise from the social context and cannot be context-free. Frake the learner among the Subanun has to grapple with problems similar to children trying to learn school subjects in our schools.

Just as we saw that 'culturally deprived' children are typified as lacking the linguistic and cognitive means to carry out abstract thought, so we find from Frake and Gladwin that it is common to characterize the thought of small-scale or simple societies as lacking the sophisticated abstractions that are the supposed pre-requisites of complex industrial societies. The argument that follows is not intended to show that the logical processes of thought in such small-scale societies correspond in any *substantive* detail to those of industrialized societies but rather that the *processes* of thought, of abstraction and theorizing are not inherently different but in many significant ways similar. The implications of this for schooling are manifold and diffuse; but it can at least be argued that all 'cultures' – class and ethnic – may have their own logics which are capable of grappling with what we shall for the moment continue to call abstract thought. On the basis of the very limited research to date, this must at least remain an open question.

It is not only, as Gladwin points out, that there are different kinds of intellectual achievement, but that the same people may be capable of achieving differently in appropriately differentiated social

occasions. It can be argued that Gladwin's wish to retain the categories of abstract and concrete seems redundant after the data he
presents. What certainly remains problematic is how the overall
plan of the Western navigator – which the Trukese is said to lack –
is turned into a course of ongoing action, how is it concretized. What
are, as Frake poses the question, the procedures for 'rules and uses'?
The description of the European navigator's procedure as deductive
does not cover in any detail the same problems of application that
Gladwin details in Trukese navigation (and so much more exhaustively in his description of Pulawat Navigation in *East is a Big Bird*).
One reason for this is presumably ignorance: there is no data on how
the European navigator proceeds in fact to navigate as a theoretical
and practical activity. Another reason is probably the assumption
that the descriptive label – deductive logic – for the procedures of
Western navigation is seen as a sufficient explanation of the achievement.

It is as though the setting out of the philosophical rules or procedures for a discipline, or the constructing of a psychological
taxonomy of cognitive levels of learning, told us something about
how students actually make what they are taught their own in an
interactive social context. Frake's data, like Labov's, suggests that
the usual simple transmission model of one to one that is implied in
most learning models is inadequate. It is inadequate in part for its
reliance on a notion that what is to be learned can be charted on a
scale of difficulty which ranges along a continuum from concrete to
abstract. This involves a complicated correspondence theory since in
some unexplicated way a child's cognitive development must be supposed to match the level of difficulty inherent in a subject or its
concepts at a given age. Both suppositions in such a correspondence
theory fail to give sufficient weight to the socially constructed man-
made nature of both ability and school – or any – knowledge.

It might be wished that schools could become more flexible in
their willingness to recognize and value the life experience that every
child brings to school, and at the same time become more willing to
examine and to justify what schooling could be about and what kind
of life experiences children are being offered.

1 William Labov
The Logic of Nonstandard English[1]

W. Labov, 'The logic of nonstandard English', *Georgetown Monographs on Language and Linguistics*, vol. 22, 1969, pp. 1–31.

In the past decade, a great deal of federally sponsored research has been devoted to the educational problems of children in ghetto schools. In order to account for the poor performance of children in these schools, educational psychologists have attempted to discover what kind of disadvantage or defect they are suffering from. The viewpoint that has been widely accepted and used as the basis for large-scale intervention programs is that the children show a cultural deficit as a result of an impoverished environment in their early years. Considerable attention has been given to language. In this area the deficit theory appears as the concept of 'verbal deprivation': Negro children from the ghetto area are said to receive little verbal stimulation, to hear very little well-formed language, and as a result are impoverished in their means of verbal expression. They cannot speak complete sentences, do not know the names of common objects, cannot form concepts or convey logical thoughts.

Unfortunately, these notions are based upon the work of educational psychologists who know very little about language and even less about Negro children. The concept of verbal deprivation has no basis in social reality: in fact, Negro children in the urban ghettos receive a great deal of verbal stimulation, hear more well-formed sentences than middle-class children, and participate fully in a highly verbal culture; they have the same basic vocabulary, possess

1. This paper was originally presented at the Twentieth Annual Georgetown Round Table Meeting on Linguistics and Language Studies, Washington, DC, 14 March 1969, where the theme was 'Linguistics and the Teaching of Standard English to Speakers of Other Languages or Dialects'.

the same capacity for conceptual learning, and use the same logic as anyone else who learns to speak and understand English.

The notion of 'verbal deprivation' is a part of the modern mythology of educational psychology, typical of the unfounded notions which tend to expand rapidly in our educational system. In past decades linguists have been as guilty as others in promoting such intellectual fashions at the expense of both teachers and children. But the myth of verbal deprivation is particularly dangerous, because it diverts attention from real defects of our educational system to imaginary defects of the child; and as we shall see, it leads its sponsors inevitably to the hypothesis of the genetic inferiority of Negro children that it was originally designed to avoid.

The most useful service which linguists can perform today is to clear away the illusion of 'verbal deprivation' and to provide a more adequate notion of the relations between standard and nonstandard dialects. In the writings of many prominent educational psychologists, we find very poor understanding of the nature of language. Children are treated as if they have no language of their own in the pre-school programs put forward by Bereiter and Engelmann (1966). The linguistic behavior of ghetto children in test situations is the principal evidence of genetic inferiority in the view of Jensen (1969). In this paper, we will examine critically both of these approaches to the language and intelligence of the populations labelled 'verbally deprived' and 'culturally deprived'[2], and attempt to explain how the myth of verbal deprivation has arisen, bringing to bear the methodological findings of sociolinguistic work and some substantive facts about language which are known to all linguists. Of particular concern is the relation between concept formation on the one hand, and dialect differences on the other, since it is in this area that the most dangerous misunderstandings are to be found.

2. I am indebted to Rosalind Weiner of the Early Childhood Education group of Operation Head Start in New York City, and to Joan Baratz of the Education Study Center, Washington, D C, for pointing out to me the scope and seriousness of the educational issues involved here, and the ways in which the cultural deprivation theory has affected federal intervention programs in recent years.

Verbality

The general setting in which the deficit theory arises consists of a number of facts which are known to all of us. One is that Negro children in the central urban ghettos do badly in all school subjects, including arithmetic and reading. In reading, they average more than two years behind the national norm (see *New York Times*, 3 December 1968). Furthermore, this lag is cumulative, so that they do worse comparatively in the fifth grade than in the first grade. Reports in the literature show that this poor performance is correlated most closely with socioeconomic status. Segregated ethnic groups seem to do worse than others – in particular, Indian, Mexican-American and Negro children. Our own work in New York City confirms that most Negro children read very poorly; however, studies in the speech community show that the situation is even worse than has been reported. If one separates the isolated and peripheral individuals from members of central peer groups, the peer-group members show even worse reading records, and to all intents and purposes are not learning to read at all during the time they spend in school (see Labov, *et al.*, 1968).

In speaking of children in the urban ghetto areas, the term 'lower class' frequently is used, as opposed to 'middle class'. In the several sociolinguistic studies we have carried out, and in many parallel studies, it has been useful to distinguish a lower-class group from a working-class one. Lower-class families are typically female-based, or matri-focal, with no father present to provide steady economic support, whereas for the working-class there is typically an intact nuclear family with the father holding a semi-skilled or skilled job. The educational problems of ghetto areas run across this important class distinction. There is no evidence, for example, that the father's presence or absence is closely correlated with educational achievement (e.g., Langer and Michaels, 1963; Coleman, *et al.*, 1966). The peer groups we have studied in south-central Harlem, representing the basic vernacular culture, include members from both family types. The attack against 'cultural deprivation' in the ghetto is overtly directed at family structures typical of lower-class families, but the educational failure we have been discussing is characteristic of both working-class and lower-class children.

This paper, therefore, will refer to children from urban ghetto areas rather than 'lower-class' children. The population we are concerned with comprises those who participate fully in the vernacular culture of the street and who have been alienated from the school system.[3] We are obviously dealing with the effects of the caste system of American society – essentially a color-marking system. Everyone recognizes this. The question is: by what mechanism does the color bar prevent children from learning to read? One answer is the notion of 'cultural deprivation' put forward by Martin Deutsch and others (Deutsch, *et al.*, 1967; Deutsch, Katz and Jensen, 1968). Negro children are said to lack the favorable factors in their home environment which enable middle-class children to do well in school. These factors involve the development of various cognitive skills through verbal interaction with adults, including the ability to reason abstractly, speak fluently and focus upon long-range goals. In their publications, these psychologists also recognize broader social factors. However, the deficit theory does not focus upon the interaction of the Negro child with white society so much as on his failure to interact with his mother at home. In the literature we find very little direct observation of verbal interaction in the Negro home. Most typically, the investigators ask the child if he has dinner with his parents, if he engages in dinner-table conversation with them, if his family takes him on trips to museums and other cultural activities, and so on. This slender thread of evidence is used to explain and interpret the large body of tests carried out in the laboratory and in the school.

The most extreme view which proceeds from this orientation – and one that is now being widely accepted – is that lower-class Negro children have no language at all. The notion is first drawn from Basil Bernstein's writings that 'much of lower-class language consists of a kind of incidental "emotional" accompaniment to action here and now' (Jensen, 1968, p. 118). Bernstein's views are filtered through a strong bias against all forms of working-class

3. The concept of nonstandard Negro English (NNE) and the vernacular culture in which it is embedded is presented in detail in Labov, *et al.* (1968, sections 1, 2, 3 and 4.1). See volume 2, section 4.3 for the linguistic traits which distinguish speakers who participate fully in the NNE culture from marginal and isolated individuals.

behavior, so that middle-class language is seen as superior in every respect – as 'more abstract, and necessarily somewhat more flexible, detailed and subtle' (p. 119). One can proceed through a range of such views until he comes to the pre-school programs of Bereiter and Engelmann (1966; Bereiter, *et al.*, 1966). Bereiter's program for an academically oriented pre-school is based upon the premise that Negro children must have a language with which they can learn and the empirical finding that these children come to school without such a language. In his work with four-year-old Negro children from Urbana, Bereiter (*et al.*, 1966, pp. 113 ff.) reports that their communication was by gestures, single words and 'a series of badly connected words or phrases', such as *They mine* and *Me got juice*. He reports that Negro children could not ask questions, that 'without exaggerating . . . these four-year-olds could make no statements of any kind'. Furthermore, when these children were asked 'Where is the book?' they did not know enough to look at the table where the book was lying in order to answer. Thus Bereiter concludes that these children's speech forms are nothing more than a series of emotional cries, and he decides to treat them 'as if the children had no language at all'. He identifies their speech with his interpretation of Bernstein's restricted code: 'the language of culturally deprived children . . . is not merely an underdeveloped version of standard English, but is a basically non-logical mode of expressive behavior' (Bereiter, *et al.*, 1966, pp. 112–13). The basic program of his pre-school is to teach them a new language devised by Engelmann, which consists of a limited series of questions and answers such as 'Where is the squirrel?' 'The squirrel is in the tree.' The children will not be punished if they use their vernacular speech on the playground, but they will not be allowed to use it in the schoolroom. If they should answer the question, 'Where is the squirrel?' with the illogical vernacular form 'In the tree' they will be reprehended by various means and made to say, 'The squirrel is in the tree.'

Linguists and psycholinguists who have worked with Negro children are apt to dismiss this view of their language as utter nonsense. Yet there is no reason to reject Bereiter's observations as spurious. They were certainly not made up. On the contrary, they give us a very clear view of the behavior of student and teacher which can be duplicated in any classroom. In our own work outside of adult-dominated environments of school and home, we have not observed Negro children behaving like this.[4] However, on many occasions we have been asked to help analyse the results of research into verbal deprivation conducted in such test situations.

Here, for example, is a complete interview with a Negro boy, one of hundreds carried out in a New York City school.[5] The boy enters a room where there is a large, friendly, white interviewer, who puts on the table in front of him a toy and says: 'Tell me everything you can about this.' (The interviewer's further remarks are in parentheses.)

[*12 seconds of silence*]
(What would you say it looks like?)
[*8 seconds of silence*]
A space ship.
(Hmmmm.)
[*13 seconds of silence*]
Like a je-et.
[*12 seconds of silence*]
Like a plane.
[*20 seconds of silence*]
(What color is it?)
Orange. [*2 seconds*] An' whi-ite. [*2 seconds*] An' green.
[*6 seconds of silence*]
(An' what could you use it for?)
[*8 seconds of silence*]
A je-et.

4. For example, in Deutsch, Katz and Jensen (1968) there is a section on Social and Psychological Perspectives which includes a chapter by Proshansky and Newton on 'The Nature and Meaning of Negro Self-Identity', and one by Rosenthal and Jacobson on 'Self-Fulfilling Prophecies in the Classroom'.

5. The research cited here was carried out in south-central Harlem and other ghetto areas in 1965–8 to describe the structural and functional differences between Negro nonstandard English and standard English in the classroom. It was supported by the Office of Education as Cooperative Research Projects 3091 and 3288. Detailed reports are given in Labov, *et al.* (1965), Labov (1967), and Labov, *et al.* (1968).

[*6 seconds of silence*]
(If you had two of them, what would you do with them?)
 [*6 seconds of silence*]
Give one to some-body.
(Hmmm. Who do you think would like to have it?)
 [*10 seconds of silence*]
Cla-rence.
(Mm. Where do you think we could get another one of these?)
At the store.
(Oh ka-ay!)

We have here the same kind of defensive, monosyllabic behavior which is reported in Bereiter's work. What is the situation that produces it? The child is in an asymmetrical situation where anything he says can literally be held against him. He has learned a number of devices to avoid saying anything in this situation, and he works very hard to achieve this end. One may observe the intonation patterns of

and

$$2 \, a \, ^3 \, \text{'o'} \, 2 \, \text{know}$$

$$a \, ^2 \, \text{space} \, ^2 \, \text{sh} \, ^3 \, \text{ip}$$

which Negro children often use when they are asked a question to which the answer is obvious. The answer may be read as: 'Will this satisfy you?'

If one takes this interview as a measure of the verbal capacity of the child, it must be as his capacity to defend himself in a hostile and threatening situation. But unfortunately, thousands of such interviews are used as evidence of the child's total verbal capacity, or more simply his verbality. It is argued that this lack of verbality explains his poor performance in school. Operation Head Start and other intervention programs have largely been based upon the deficit theory – the notions that such interviews give us a measure of the child's verbal capacity and that the verbal stimulation which he has been missing can be supplied in a pre-school environment.

The verbal behavior which is shown by the child in the situation quoted above is not the result of the ineptness of the interviewer. It is rather the result of regular sociolinguistic factors operating upon adult and child in this asymmetrical situation. In our work in urban

ghetto areas, we have often encountered such behavior. Ordinarily
we worked with boys ten to seventeen years old, and whenever we
extended our approach downward to eight- or nine-year-olds, we
began to see the need for different techniques to explore the verbal
capacity of the child. At one point we began a series of interviews
with younger brothers of the Thunderbirds in 1390 Fifth Avenue [a
pre-adolescent group studied in this research]. Clarence Robins returned after an interview with eight-year-old Leon L., who showed
the following minimal response to topics which arouse intense
interest in other interviews with older boys.

CR What if you saw somebody kickin' somebody else on the ground,
   or was using a stick, what would you do if you saw that?
LEON Mmmm.
CR If it was supposed to be a fair fight –
LEON I don' know.
CR You don't know? Would you do anything? ... huh? I can't hear
   you.
LEON No.
CR Did you ever see somebody got beat up real bad?
LEON ... Nope ...
CR Well – uh – did you ever get into a fight with a guy?
LEON Nope.
CR That was bigger than you?
LEON Nope.
CR You never been in a fight?
LEON Nope ...
CR Nobody ever pick on you?
LEON Nope.
CR Nobody ever hit you?
LEON Nope.
CR How come?
LEON Ah 'on' know.
CR Didn't you ever hit somebody?
LEON Nope.
CR (*incredulously*) You never hit nobody?
LEON Mhm.
CR Aww, ba-a-abe, you ain't gonna tell me that!

It may be that Leon is here defending himself against accusations of wrong-doing, since Clarence knows that Leon has been in fights, that he has been taking pencils away from little boys, and so on. But if we turn to a more neutral subject, we find the same pattern:

CR You watch – you like to watch television? . . . Hey, Leon . . . you like to watch television? (*Leon nods*) What's your favorite program?

LEON Uhhmmmm . . . I look at cartoons.

CR Well, what's your favorite one? What's your favorite program?

LEON Superman . . .

CR Yeah? Did you see Superman – ah – yesterday, or day before yesterday? When's the last time you saw Superman?

LEON Sa-aturday . . .

CR You rem – you saw it Saturday? What was the story all about? You remember the story?

LEON Mm.

CR You don't remember the story of what – that you saw of Superman?

LEON Nope.

CR You don't remember what happened, huh?

LEON Hm-m.

CR I see – ah – what other stories do you like to watch on TV ?

LEON Mmmm? . . . umm . . . (*glottalization*)

CR Hmm? (*four seconds*)

LEON Hh?

CR What's th' other stories that you like to watch?

LEON Mi-ighty Mouse . . .

CR And what else?

LEON Ummmm . . . ahm . . .

This nonverbal behavior occurs in a relatively favorable context for adult–child interaction. The adult is a Negro man raised in Harlem, who knows this particular neighborhood and these boys very well. He is a skilled interviewer who has obtained a very high level of verbal response with techniques developed for a different age level, and he has an extraordinary advantage over most teachers or experimenters in these respects. But even his skills and personality are ineffective in breaking down the social constraints that prevail here.

When we reviewed the record of this interview with Leon, we decided to use it as a test of our own knowledge of the sociolinguistic factors which control speech. In the next interview with Leon we made the following changes in the social situation:

1. Clarence brought along a supply of potato chips, changing the interview into something more in the nature of a party.

2. He brought along Leon's best friend, eight-year-old Gregory.

3. We reduced the height in balance by having Clarence get down on the floor of Leon's room; he dropped from six feet, two inches to three feet, six inches.

4. Clarence introduced taboo words and taboo topics, and proved, to Leon's surprise, that one can say anything into our microphone without any fear of retaliation.

The result of these changes is a striking difference in the volume and style of speech.

CR Is there anybody who says *your momma drink pee?*

LEON (*rapidly and breathlessly*) Yee-ah!

GREG Yup!

LEON: And *your father eat doo-doo for breakfas'!*

CR Ohhh! ! (*laughs*)

LEON And they say your father — *your father eat doo-doo for dinner!*

GREG When they sound on me, I say *CBS.*

CR What that mean?

⌠LEON Congo booger-snatch! (*laughs*)

⌡GREG Congo booger-snatcher! (*laughs*)

GREG And sometimes I'll curse with *BB.*

CR What that?

GREG Black boy! (*Leon — crunching on potato chips*) Oh that's a *MBB.*

CR *MBB.* What's that?

GREG 'Merican Black Boy.

CR Oh ...

GREG Anyway, 'Mericans is same like white people, right?

LEON And they talk about Allah.

CR Oh yeah?

GREG Yeah.

CR What they say about Allah?

⎧ LEON Allah – Allah is God.

⎩ GREG Allah –

CR And what else?

LEON I don' know the res'.

GREG Allah i – Allah is God, Allah is the only God, Allah . . .

LEON Allah is the *son* of God.

GREG But can he make magic?

LEON Nope.

GREG I know who can make magic.

CR Who can?

LEON The God, the *real* one.

CR Who can make magic?

GREG The son of po' – [CR Hm?] I'm sayin' the po'k chop God![6] He only a po'k chop God! (*Leon chuckles*).

(The 'nonverbal' Leon is now competing actively for the floor; Gregory and Leon talk to each other as much as they do to the interviewer.)

We can make a more direct comparison of the two interviews by examining the section on fighting. Leon persists in denying that he fights, but he can no longer use monosyllabic answers, and Gregory cuts through his façade in a way that Clarence Robins alone was unable to do.

CR Now, you said you had this fight, now, but I wanted you to tell me about the fight that you had.

LEON I ain't had no fight.

⎧ GREG Yes, you did!   He said Barry,

⎩ CR You said you had one! you had a fight with Butchie,

6. The reference to the *pork chop God* condenses several concepts of black nationalism current in the Harlem community. A *pork chop* is a Negro who has not lost the traditional subservient ideology of the South, who has no knowledge of himself in Muslim terms, and the *pork chop God* would be the traditional God of Southern Baptists. He and His followers may be pork chops, but He still holds the power in Leon and Gregory's world.

GREG   An' he say Garland . . . an' Michael.

CR an' Barry . . .

LEON I di'n'; you said that, Gregory!

GREG   You did.

LEON You know you said that!

GREG   You said Garland, remember that?

GREG You said Garland!   Yes you did!

CR   You said Garland, that's right.

GREG He said Mich – an' I say Michael.

CR Did you have a fight with Garland?

LEON   Uh-uh.

CR You had one, and he beat you up, too!

GREG Yes he did!

LEON No, I di – I never had a fight with Butch! . . .

The same pattern can be seen on other local topics, where the interviewer brings neighborhood gossip to bear on Leon and Gregory acts as a witness.

CR . . . Hey Gregory! I heard that around here . . . and I'm 'on' tell you who said it, too . . .

LEON   Who?

CR about you . . .

LEON   Who?

GREG   I'd say it!

CR They said that – they say that the only person you play with is David Gilbert.

LEON Yee-ah! yee-ah! yee-ah! . . .

GREG   That's who you play with!

LEON I 'on' play with him no more!

GREG   Yes you do!

LEON I 'on' play with him no more!

GREG But remember, about me and Robbie?

LEON So that's not –

GREG and you went to Petey and Gilbert's house, 'member?
     Ah haaah!!

LEON So that's – so – but I would – I had came back out, an' I ain't go to his house no more . . .

The observer must now draw a very different conclusion about the verbal capacity of Leon. The monosyllabic speaker who had nothing to say about anything and cannot remember what he did yesterday has disappeared. Instead, we have two boys who have so much to say they keep interrupting each other, who seem to have no difficulty in using the English language to express themselves. And we in turn obtain the volume of speech and the rich array of grammatical devices which we need for analyzing the structure of non-standard Negro English (NNE): negative concord [*I 'on' play with him no more*], the pluperfect [*had came back out*], negative perfect [*I ain't had*], the negative preterite [*I ain't go*], and so on.

We can now transfer this demonstration of the sociolinguistic control of speech to other test situations – including IQ and reading tests in school. It should be immediately apparent that none of the standard tests will come anywhere near measuring Leon's verbal capacity. On these tests he will show up as very much the monosyllabic, inept, ignorant, bumbling child of our first interview. The teacher has far less ability than Clarence Robins to elicit speech from this child; Clarence knows the community, the things that Leon has been doing, and the things that Leon would like to talk about. But the power relationships in a one-to-one confrontation between adult and child are too asymmetrical. This does not mean that some Negro children will not talk a great deal when alone with an adult, or that an adult cannot get close to any child. It means that the social situation is the most powerful determinant of verbal behavior and that an adult must enter into the right social relation with a child if he wants to find out what a child can do: this is just what many teachers cannot do.

The view of the Negro speech community which we obtain from our work in the ghetto areas is precisely the opposite from that reported by Deutsch, Engelmann and Bereiter. We see a child bathed in verbal stimulation from morning to night. We see many speech events which depend upon the competitive exhibition of verbal skills: sounding, singing, toasts, rifting, louding – a whole range of activities in which the individual gains status through his use of language (see Labov, *et al.*, 1968, section 4.2). We see the younger child trying to acquire these skills from older children – hanging around on the outskirts of the older peer group, and imitating this behavior to the best of his ability. We see no connection between verbal skill at the speech events characteristic of the street culture and success in the schoolroom.

Verbosity

There are undoubtedly many verbal skills which children from ghetto areas must learn in order to do well in the school situation, and some of these are indeed characteristic of middle-class verbal behavior. Precision in spelling, practice in handling abstract symbols, the ability to state explicitly the meaning of words, and a richer knowledge of the Latinate vocabulary, may all be useful acquisitions. But is it true that *all* of the middle-class verbal habits are functional and desirable in the school situation? Before we impose middle-class verbal style upon children from other cultural groups, we should find out how much of this is useful for the main work of analysing and generalizing, and how much is merely stylistic – or even dysfunctional. In high school and college middle-class children spontaneously complicate their syntax to the point that instructors despair of getting them to make their language simpler and clearer. In every learned journal one can find examples of jargon and empty elaboration – and complaints about it. Is the 'elaborate code' of Bernstein really so 'flexible, detailed and subtle' as some psychologists believe? (Jensen, 1969, p. 119) Isn't it also turgid, redundant, and empty? Is it not simply an elaborated *style*, rather than a superior code or system?[7]

Our work in the speech community makes it painfully obvious that in many ways working-class speakers are more effective narrators, reasoners and debaters than many middle-class speakers who temporize, qualify, and lose their argument in a mass of irrelevant detail. Many academic writers try to rid themselves of that part of

7. The term *code* is central in Bernstein's description of the differences between working-class and middle-class styles of speech. The restrictions and elaborations of speech observed are labelled as 'codes' to indicate the principles governing selection from the range of possible English sentences. No rules or detailed description of the operation of such codes are provided as yet, so that this central concept remains to be specified.

middle-class style that is empty pretension, and keep that part that is needed for precision. But the average middle-class speaker that we encounter makes no such effort; he is enmeshed in verbiage, the victim of sociolinguistic factors beyond his control.

I will not attempt to support this argument here with systematic quantitative evidence, although it is possible to develop measures which show how far middle-class speakers can wander from the point. I would like to contrast two speakers dealing with roughly the same topic — matters of belief. The first is Larry H., a fifteen-year-old core member of the Jets, being interviewed by John Lewis. Larry is one of the loudest and roughest members of the Jets, one who gives the least recognition to the conventional rules of politeness.[8] For most readers of this paper, first contact with Larry would produce some fairly negative reactions on both sides: it is probable that you would not *like* him any more than his teachers do. Larry causes trouble in and out of school; he was put back from the eleventh grade to the ninth, and has been threatened with further action by the school authorities.

JL What happens to you after you die? Do you know?

LARRY Yeah, I know.

JL What?

LARRY After they put you in the ground, your body turns into — ah — bones, an' shit.

JL What happens to your spirit?

LARRY Your spirit — soon as you die, your spirit leaves you.

JL And where does the spirit go?

LARRY Well, it all depends . . .

JL On what?

LARRY You know, like some people say if you're good an' shit, your spirit goin' t'heaven . . . 'n' if you bad, your spirit goin' to hell. Well, bullshit! Your spirit goin' to hell anyway, good or bad.

8. A direct view of Larry's verbal style in a hostile encounter is given in Labov, *et al.* (1968), vol. 2, pp. 39–43. Gray's Oral Reading Test was being given to a group of Jets on the steps of a brownstone house in Harlem, and the landlord tried unsuccessfully to make the Jets move. Larry's verbal style in this encounter matches the reports he gives of himself in a number of narratives cited in section 4.8.

JL Why?

LARRY Why? I'll tell you why. 'Cause, you see, doesn' nobody really know that it's a God, y'know, 'cause I mean I have seen black gods, pink gods, white gods, all color gods, and don't nobody know it's really a God. An' when they be sayin' if you good, you goin' t'heaven, tha's bullshit, 'cause you ain't goin' to no heaven, 'cause it ain't no heaven for you to go to.

Larry is a paradigmatic speaker of nonstandard Negro English (NNE) as opposed to standard English. His grammar shows a high concentration of such characteristic NNE forms as negative inversion [*don't nobody know . . .*], negative concord [*you ain't goin' to no heaven . . .*], invariant *be* [*when they be sayin' . . .*], dummy *it* for standard English *there* [*it ain't no heaven . . .*], optional copula deletion [*if you're good . . . if you bad . . .*], and full forms of auxiliaries [*I have seen . . .*]. The only standard English influence in this passage is the one case of *doesn't* instead of the invariant *don't* of NNE. Larry also provides a paradigmatic example of the rhetorical style of NNE: he can sum up a complex argument in a few words, and the full force of his opinions comes through without qualification or reservation. He is eminently quotable, and his interviews give us many concise statements of the NNE point of view. One can almost say that Larry *speaks* the NNE culture (see Labov, *et al.*, 1968, vol. 2, pp. 38, 71–3, 291–2).

It is the logical form of this passage which is of particular interest here. Larry presents a complex set of interdependent propositions which can be explicated by setting out the standard English equivalents in linear order. The basic argument is to deny the twin propositions

(A) If you are good,   (B) then your spirit will go to heaven.
(−A) If you are bad,   (C) then your spirit will go to hell.

Larry denies (B), and asserts that *if* (A) *or* (−A), *then* (C). His argument may be outlined as follows:

1. Everyone has a different idea of what God is like.
2. Therefore nobody really knows that God exists.
3. If there is a heaven, it was made by God.

4. If God doesn't exist, he couldn't have made heaven.
5. Therefore heaven does not exist.
6. You can't go somewhere that doesn't exist.
—B. Therefore you can't go to heaven.
C. Therefore you are going to hell.

The argument is presented in the order: (C), because (2) because (1), therefore (2), therefore (—B) because (5) and (6). Part of the argument is implicit: the connection (2) therefore (—B) leaves unstated the connecting links (3) and (4), and in this interval Larry strengthens the propositions from the form (2) *Nobody knows if there is* . . . to (5) *There is no*. . . . Otherwise, the case is presented explicitly as well as economically. The complex argument is summed up in Larry's last sentence, which shows formally the dependence of (—B) on (5) and (6).

An' when they be sayin' if you good, you goin' t'heaven,
[*The proposition, if* (A), *then* (B)]
Tha's bullshit,
[*is absurd*]
'cause you ain't goin' to no heaven
[*because* (—B)]
'cause it ain't no heaven for you to go to.
[*because* (5) *and* (6)].

This hypothetical argument is not carried on at a high level of seriousness. It is a game played with ideas as counters, in which opponents use a wide variety of verbal devices to win. There is no personal commitment to any of these propositions, and no reluctance to strengthen one's argument by bending the rules of logic as in the (2–5) sequence. But if the opponent invokes the rules of logic, they hold. In John Lewis' interviews, he often makes this move, and the force of his argument is always acknowledged and countered within the rules of logic. In this case, he pointed out the fallacy that the argument (2–3–4–5–6) leads to (—C) as well as (—B), so it cannot be used to support Larry's assertion (C):

JL Well, if there's no heaven, how could there be a hell?
LARRY I mean – ye – eah. Well, let me tell you, it ain't no hell, 'cause this is hell right here, y'know!

JL This is hell?

LARRY Yeah, this is hell right here!

Larry's answer is quick, ingenious and decisive. The application of
the (3–4–5) argument to hell is denied, since hell is here, and therefore conclusion (C) stands. These are not ready-made or pre-
conceived opinions, but new propositions devised to win the logical
argument in the game being played. The reader will note the speed
and precision of Larry's mental operations. He does not wander, or
insert meaningless verbiage. The only repetition is (2), placed before
and after (1) in his original statement. It is often said that the
nonstandard vernacular is not suited for dealing with abstract or
hypothetical questions, but in fact speakers from the NNE community take great delight in exercising their wit and logic on
the most improbable and problematical matters. Despite the fact
that Larry H. does not believe in God, and has just denied all
knowledge of him, John Lewis advances the following hypothetical
question:

JL . . . But, just say that there is a God, what color is he? White or
   black?

LARRY Well, if it is a God . . . I wouldn' know what color, I
   couldn' say, – couldn' nobody say what color he is or really
   would be.

JL But now, jus' suppose there was a God –

LARRY Unless'n they say . . .

JL No, I was jus' sayin' jus' suppose there is a God, would he be
   white or black?

LARRY . . . He'd be white, man.

JL Why?

LARRY Why? I'll tell you why. 'Cause the average whitey out here
   got everything, you dig? And the nigger ain't got shit, y'know?
   Y'understan'? So – um – for – in order for *that* to happen, you
   know it ain't no black God that's doin' that bullshit.

No one can hear Larry's answer to this question without being con-
vinced that they are in the presence of a skilled speaker with great
'verbal presence of mind', who can use the English language expertly
for many purposes. Larry's answer to John Lewis is again a complex

argument. The formulation is not standard English, but it is clear and effective even for those not familiar with the vernacular. The nearest standard English equivalent might be: 'So you know that God isn't black, because if he was, he wouldn't have arranged things like that.'

The reader will have noted that this analysis is being carried out in standard English, and the inevitable challenge is: why not write in NNE, then, or in your own nonstandard dialect? The fundamental reason is, of course, one of firmly fixed social conventions. All communities agree that standard English is the 'proper' medium for formal writing and public communication. Furthermore, it seems likely that standard English has an advantage over NNE in explicit analysis of surface forms, which is what we are doing here. We will return to this opposition between explicitness and logical statement in subsequent sections on grammaticality and logic. First, however, it will be helpful to examine standard English in its primary natural setting, as the medium for informal spoken communication of middle-class speakers.

Let us now turn to the second speaker, an upper-middle-class, college educated Negro man being interviewed by Clarence Robins in our survey of adults in Central Harlem.

CR Do you know of anything that someone can do, to have someone who has passed on visit him in a dream?

CHARLES M. Well, I even heard my parents say that there is such a thing as something in dreams some things like that, and sometimes dreams do come true. I have personally never had a dream come true. I've never dreamt that somebody was dying and they actually died, (Mhm) or that I was going to have ten dollars the next day and somehow I got ten dollars in my pocket. (Mhm). I don't particularly believe in that, I don't think it's true. I do feel, though, that there is such a thing as – ah – witchcraft. I do feel that in certain cultures there is such a thing as witchcraft, or some sort of *science* of witchcraft; I don't think that it's just a matter of believing hard enough that there is such a thing as witchcraft. I do believe that there is such a thing that a person can put himself in a state of *mind* (Mhm), or that – er – something could be given them to intoxicate them in a certain – to a certain frame of mind – that – that could actually be considered witch-craft.

Charles M. is obviously a 'good speaker' who strikes the listener as well-educated, intelligent and sincere. He is a likeable and attractive person – the kind of person that middle-class listeners rate very high on a scale of 'job suitability' and equally high as a potential friend.[9] His language is more moderate and tempered than Larry's; he makes every effort to qualify his opinions, and seems anxious to avoid any mis-statements or over-statements. From these qualities emerge the primary characteristic of this passage – its *verbosity*. Words multiply, some modifying and qualifying, others repeating or padding the main argument. The first half of this extract is a re-sponse to the initial question on dreams, basically:

1. Some people say that dreams sometimes come true.
2. I have never had a dream come true.
3. Therefore I don't believe (1).

Some characteristic filler phrases appear here: *such a thing as, some things like that, particularly*. Two examples of dreams given after (2) are afterthoughts that might have been given after (1). Prop-osition (3) is stated twice for no obvious reason. Nevertheless, this much of Charles M.'s response is well-directed to the point of the question. He then volunteers a statement of his beliefs about witch-craft which shows the difficulty of middle-class speakers who (a) want to express a belief in something but (b) want to show them-selves as judicious, rational and free from superstitions. The basic proposition can be stated simply in five words:

But I believe in witchcraft.

However, the idea is enlarged to exactly a hundred words, and it is difficult to see what else is being said. In the following quotations, padding which can be removed without change in meaning is shown in brackets.

1. 'I [do] feel, though, that there is [such a thing as] witchcraft.' *Feel* seems to be a euphemism for 'believe'.

9. For a description of subjective reaction tests which utilize these evaluate dimensions, see Labov, *et al.* (1968, section 4.6).

2. '[I do feel that] in certain cultures [there is such a thing as witch-craft.]' This repetition seems designed only to introduce the word *culture*, which lets us know that the speaker knows about anthropology. Does *certain cultures* mean 'not in ours' or 'not in all'?

3. '[or some sort of *science* of witchcraft.]' This addition seems to have no clear meaning at all. What is a 'science' of witchcraft as opposed to just plain witchcraft?[10] The main function is to introduce the word *science*, though it seems to have no connection to what follows.

4. 'I don't think that it's just [a matter of] believing hard enough that [there is such a thing as] witchcraft.' The speaker argues that witchcraft is not merely a belief; there is more to it.

5. 'I [do] believe that [*there is such a thing that*] a person can put himself in a state of *mind* ... that [*could actually be considered*] witchcraft.' Is witchcraft as a state of mind different from the state of belief denied in (4)?

6. 'or that something could be given them to intoxicate them [to a certain frame of mind] ...' The third learned word, *intoxicate*, is introduced by this addition. The vacuity of this passage becomes more evident if we remove repetitions, fashionable words and stylistic decorations:

But I believe in witchcraft.
I don't think witchcraft is just a belief.
A person can put himself or be put in a state of mind that is witchcraft.

Without the extra verbiage and the OK words like *science, culture* and *intoxicate*, Charles M. appears as something less than a first-rate thinker. The initial impression of him as a good speaker is simply our long-conditioned reaction to middle-class verbosity: we know that people who use these stylistic devices are educated

10. Several middle-class readers of this page have suggested that *science* here refers to some form of control as opposed to belief; the 'science of witchcraft' would then be a kind of engineering of mental states; other interpretations can of course be provided. The fact remains that no such subtleties of interpretation are needed to understand Larry's remarks.

people, and we are inclined to credit them with saying something intelligent. Our reactions are accurate in one sense: Charles M. is more educated than Larry. But is he more rational, more logical, or more intelligent? Is he any better at thinking out a problem to its solution? Does he deal more easily with abstractions? There is no reason to think so. Charles M. succeeds in letting us know that he is educated, but in the end we do not know what he is trying to say, and neither does he.

In the previous section I have attempted to explain the origin of the myth that lower-class Negro children are nonverbal. The examples just given may help to account for the corresponding myth that middle-class language is in itself better suited for dealing with abstract, logically complex and hypothetical questions. These examples are intended to have a certain negative force. They are not controlled experiments: on the contrary, this and the preceding section are designed to convince the reader that the controlled experiments that have been offered in evidence are misleading. The only thing that is 'controlled' is the superficial form of the stimulus: all children are asked 'What do you think of capital punishment?' or 'Tell me everything you can about this.' But the speaker's interpretation of these requests, and the action he believes is appropriate in response is completely uncontrolled. One can view these test stimuli as requests for information, commands for action, as threats of punishment, or as meaningless sequences of words. They are probably intended as something altogether different: as requests for display;[11] but in any case the experimenter is normally unaware of the problem of interpretation. The methods of educational psychologists like Deutsch, Jensen and Bereiter follow the pattern designed for animal experiments where motivation is controlled by such simple methods as withholding food until a certain weight reduction is reached. With human subjects, it is absurd to believe that an identical 'stimulus' is obtained by asking everyone the 'same question'.

Since the crucial intervening variables of interpretation and motivation are uncontrolled, most of the literature on verbal deprivation tells us nothing about the capacities of children. They

11. The concept of a 'request for verbal display' is here drawn from a treatment of the therapeutic interview given by Blum (1970).

are only the trappings of science: an approach which substitutes the formal procedures of the scientific method for the activity itself. With our present limited grasp of these problems, the best we can do to understand the verbal capacities of children is to study them within the cultural context in which they were developed.

It is not only the NNE vernacular which should be studied in this way, but also the language of middle-class children. The explicitness and precision which we hope to gain from copying middle-class forms are often the product of the test situation, and limited to it. For example, it was stated in the first part of this paper that working-class children hear more well-formed sentences than middle-class children. This statement may seem extraordinary in the light of the current belief of many linguists that most people do not speak in well-formed sentences, and that their actual speech production or 'performance' is ungrammatical.[12] But those who have worked with any body of natural speech know that this is not the case. Our own studies (Labov, 1966) of the grammaticality of every-day speech show that the great majority of utterances in all contexts are complete sentences, and most of the rest can be reduced to grammatical form by the small set of 'editing rules'. The proportions of grammatical sentences vary with class backgrounds and styles. The highest percentage of well-formed sentences are found in casual speech, and working-class speakers use more well-formed sentences than middle-class speakers. The widespread myth that most speech is ungrammatical is no doubt based upon tapes made at learned conferences, where we obtain the maximum number of irreducibly ungrammatical sequences.

It is true that technical and scientific books are written in a style

12. In a number of presentations, Chomsky has asserted that the great majority of the sentences which a child hears are ungrammatical (95 per cent). Chomsky (1965, p. 58), presents this notion as one of the arguments in his general statement of the 'nativist' position: 'A consideration of the character of the grammar that is acquired, *the degenerate quality and narrowly limited extent of the available data* [my emphasis], the striking uniformity of the resulting grammars, and their independence of intelligence, motivation, and emotional state, over wide ranges of variation, leave little hope that much of the structure of the language can be learned. . . .'

which is markedly 'middle-class'. But unfortunately, we often fail to achieve the explicitness and precision which we look for in such writing; and the speech of many middle-class people departs maximally from this target. All too often, standard English is represented by a style that is simultaneously over-particular and vague. The accumulating flow of words buries rather than strikes the target. It is this verbosity which is most easily taught and most easily learned, so that words take the place of thought, and nothing can be found behind them.

When Bernstein (1966, for example) describes his 'elaborated code' in general terms, it emerges as a subtle and sophisticated mode of planning utterances, achieving structural variety, taking the other person's knowledge into account, and so on. But when it comes to describing the actual difference between middle-class and working-class speakers (Bernstein, 1966), we are presented with a proliferation of 'I think', of the passive, of modals and auxiliaries, of the first person pronoun, of uncommon words; these are the bench marks of hemming and hawing, backing and filling, that are used by Charles M., devices which often obscure whatever positive contribution education can make to our use of language. When we have discovered how much middle-class style is a matter of fashion and how much actually helps us express our ideas clearly, we will have done ourselves a great service. We will then be in a position to say what standard grammatical rules must be taught to nonstandard speakers in the early grades.

Grammaticality

Let us now examine Bereiter's own data on the verbal behavior of the children he dealt with. The expressions *They mine* and *Me got juice* are cited as examples of a language which lacks the means for expressing logical relations – in this case characterized as 'a series of badly connected words' (Bereiter, *et al.*, 1966, pp. 113 ff.). In the case of *They mine*, it is apparent that Bereiter confuses the notions of logic and explicitness. We know that there are many languages of the world which do not have a present copula, and which conjoin subject and predicate complement without a verb. Russian, Hungarian and Arabic may be foreign; but they are not by that same token illogical. In the case of NNE we are not dealing with even this superficial grammatical difference, but rather with a low-level rule which carries contraction one step farther to delete single consonants representing the verbs *is, have*, or *will* (Labov, 1969). We have yet to find any children who do not sometimes use the full forms of *is* and *will*, even though they may frequently delete it. Our recent studies with Negro children four to seven years old indicate that they use the full form of the copula *is* more often than preadolescents ten to twelve years old, or the adolescents fourteen to seventeen years old.[13]

Furthermore, the deletion of the *is* or *are* in NNE is not the result of erratic or illogical behavior: it follows the same regular rules as standard English contraction. Wherever standard English can contract, Negro children use either the contracted form or (more commonly) the deleted zero form. Thus *They mine* corresponds to standard *They're mine*, not to the full form *They are mine*. On the other hand, no such deletion is possible in positions where standard English cannot contract: just as one cannot say *That's what they're* in standard English, *That's what they* is equally impossible in the vernacular we are considering. The internal constraints upon both of these rules show that we are dealing with a phonological process like contraction, sensitive to such phonetic conditions as whether or not the next word begins with a vowel or a consonant. The appropriate use of the deletion rule, like the contraction rule, requires a deep and intimate knowledge of English grammar and phonology. Such knowledge is not available for conscious inspection by native speakers. The rules we have recently worked out for standard contraction (Labov, 1969) have never appeared in any grammar, and are certainly not a part of the conscious knowledge of any standard English speakers. Nevertheless, the adult or child who uses these rules must have formed at some level of psychological organization clear concepts of 'tense marker', 'verb phrase', 'rule ordering', 'sentence embedding', 'pronoun' and many other grammatical categories which are essential parts of any logical system.

13. This is from work on the grammars and comprehension of Negro children, four to eight years old, being carried out by Professor Jane Torrey of Connecticut College in extension of the research cited above in Labov, *et al.* (1968).

Bereiter's reaction to the sentence *Me got juice* is even more puzzling. If Bereiter believes that *Me got juice* is not a logical expression, it can only be that he interprets the use of the objective pronoun *me* as representing a difference in logical relationship to the verb: that the child is in fact saying that *the juice got him* rather than *he got the juice*! If on the other hand the child means *I got juice*, then this sentence form shows only that he has not learned the formal rules for the use of the subjective form *I* and oblique form *me*. We have in fact encountered many children who do not have these formal rules in order at the ages of four, five, six or even eight. It is extremely difficult to construct a minimal pair to show that the difference between *he* and *him,* or *she* and *her*, carries cognitive meaning. In almost every case, it is the context which tells us who is the agent and who is acted upon. We must then ask: what differences in cognitive, structural orientation are signalled by the fact that the child has not learned this formal rule? In the tests carried out by Jane Torrey it is evident that the children concerned do understand the difference in meaning between *she* and *her* when another person uses the forms; all that remains is that the children themselves do not use the two forms. Our knowledge of the cognitive correlates of grammatical differences is certainly in its infancy; for this is one of very many questions which we simply cannot answer. At the moment we do not know how to construct any kind of experiment which would lead to an answer; we do not even know what type of cognitive correlate we would be looking for.

Bereiter shows even more profound ignorance of the rules of discourse and of syntax when he rejects *In the tree* as an illogical, or badly-formed answer to *Where is the squirrel?* Such elliptical answers are of course used by everyone; they show the appropriate deletion of subject and main verb, leaving the locative which is questioned by *wh + there*. The reply *In the tree* demonstrates that the listener has been attentive to and apprehended the syntax of the speaker.[14] Whatever formal structure we wish to write for expressions such as *Yes* or *Home* or *In the tree*, it is obvious that they cannot be interpreted without knowing the structure of the question

14. The attention to the speaker's syntax required of the listener is analysed in detail by Professor Harvey Sacks in his unpublished 1968 lectures.

which preceded them, and that they presuppose an understanding of the syntax of the question. Thus if you ask me 'Where is the squirrel?' it is necessary for me to understand the processes of *wh*-attachment, *wh*-attraction to the front of the sentence, and flip-flop of auxiliary and subject to produce this sentence from an underlying form which would otherwise have produced *The squirrel is there*. If the child had answered *The tree*, or *Squirrel the tree*, or *The in tree*, we would then assume that he did not understand the syntax of the full form, *The squirrel is in the tree*. Given the data that Bereiter presents, we cannot conclude that the child has no grammar, but only that the investigator does not understand the rules of grammar. It does not necessarily do any harm to use the full form *The squirrel is in the tree*, if one wants to make fully explicit the rules of grammar which the child has internalized. Much of logical analysis consists of making explicit just that kind of internalized rule. But it is hard to believe that any good can come from a program which begins with so many misconceptions about the input data. Bereiter and Engelmann believe that in teaching the child to say *The squirrel is in the tree* or *This is a box* and *This is not a box* they are teaching him an entirely new language, whereas in fact they are only teaching him to produce slightly different forms of the language he already has.

Logic

For many generations American schoolteachers have devoted themselves to correcting a small number of nonstandard English rules to their standard equivalents under the impression that they were teaching logic. This view has been reinforced and given theoretical justification by the claim that NNE lacks the means for the expression of logical thought.

Let us consider for a moment the possibility that Negro children do not operate with the same logic that middle-class adults display. This would inevitably mean that sentences of a certain grammatical form would have different truth values for the two types of speakers. One of the most obvious places to look for such a difference is in the handling of the negative, and here we encounter one of the nonstandard items which has been stigmatized as illogical by schoolteachers – the double negative, or as we term it, negative concord. A child who says *He don't know nothing* is often said to be making an illogical statement without knowing it. According to the teacher, the child wants to say *He knows nothing* but puts in an extra negative without realizing it, and so conveys the opposite meaning, *He does not know nothing*, which reduces to *He knows something*. I need not emphasize that this is an absurd interpretation. If a nonstandard speaker wishes to say that *He does not know nothing*, he does so by simply placing contrastive stress on both negatives as I have done here (*He don't know nothing*) indicating that they are derived from two underlying negatives in the deep structure. But note that the middle-class speaker does exactly the same thing when he wants to signal the existence of two underlying negatives: *He doesn't know nothing*. In the standard form with one underlying negative (*He doesn't know anything*), the indefinite *anything* contains the same superficial reference to a preceding negative in the surface structure as the nonstandard *nothing* does. In the corresponding positive sentence, the indefinite *something* is used. The dialect difference, like most of the differences between the standard and nonstandard forms, is one of surface form, and has nothing to do with the underlying logic of the sentence.

We can summarize the ways in which the two dialects differ:

	Standard English, SE	Nonstandard Negro English, NNE
Positive:	*He knows something*	*He know something*
Negative:	*He doesn't know anything*	*He don't know nothing*
Double negative:	*He doesn't know nothing*	*He don't know nothing*

This array makes it plain that the only difference between the two dialects is in superficial form. When a single negative is found in the deep structure, standard English converts *something* to the indefinite *anything*; NNE converts it to *nothing*. When speakers want to signal the presence of two negatives, they do it in the same way. No one would have any difficulty constructing the same table of truth values for both dialects. English is a rare language in its insistence that the negative particle be incorporated in the first indefinite only. The Anglo-Saxon authors of the Peterborough Chronicle were surely not illogical when they wrote *For ne waeren nan martyrs swa pined alse he waeron,* literally, 'For never weren't no martyrs so tortured as these were.' The 'logical' forms of current standard English are simply the accepted conventions of our present-day formal style. Russian, Spanish, French and Hungarian show the same negative concord as nonstandard English, and they are surely not illogical in this. What is termed 'logical' in standard English is of course the conventions which are habitual. The distribution of negative concord in English dialects can be summarized in this way (Labov, *et al.,* 1968, section 3.6; Labov, 1968):

1. In all dialects of English, the negative is attracted to a lone indefinite before the verb: *Nobody knows anything,* not *Anybody doesn't know anything.*

2. In some nonstandard white dialects, the negative also combines optionally with all other indefinites: *Nobody knows nothing, He never took none of them.*

3. In other white nonstandard dialects, the negative may also appear in pre-verbal position in the same clause: *Nobody doesn't know nothing.*

4. In nonstandard Negro English, negative concord is obligatory to all indefinites within the clause, and it may even be added to pre-verbal position in following clauses: *Nobody didn't know he didn't* (meaning, *Nobody knew he did*).

Thus all dialects of English share a categorical rule which attracts the negative to an indefinite subject, and they merely differ in the extent to which the negative particle is also distributed to other indefinites in pre-verbal position. It would have been impossible for us to arrive at this analysis if we did not know that Negro speakers are using the same underlying logic as everyone else.

Negative concord is more firmly established in nonstandard Negro English than in other nonstandard dialects. The white nonstandard speaker shows variation in this rule, saying one time, *Nobody ever goes there* and the next *Nobody never goes there.* Core speakers of the NNE vernacular consistently use the latter form. In repetition tests which we conducted with adolescent Negro boys (Labov, *et al.*, 1968, section 3.9), standard forms were repeated with negative concord. Here, for example, are three trials by two thirteen-year-old members (Boot and David) of the Thunderbirds.

MODEL BY INTERVIEWER:
Nobody ever sat at any of those desks, anyhow.

BOOT:
1. Nobody never sa-No [whitey] never sat at any o' tho' dess, anyhow.
2. Nobody never sat any any o' tho' dess, anyhow.
3. Nobody as ever sat at no desses, anyhow.

DAVID:
1. Nobody ever sat in-in-in-in- none o' – say it again?
2. Nobody never sat in none o' tho' desses anyhow.
3. Nobody -aww! Nobody never ex- Dawg!

It can certainly be said that Boot and David fail the test; they have not repeated the sentence correctly – that is, word for word. But have they failed because they could not grasp the meaning of the sentence? The situation is in fact just the opposite; they failed because they perceived only the meaning and not the superficial form. Boot and David are typical of many speakers who do not perceive the surface details of the utterance so much as the underlying semantic structure, which they unhesitatingly translate into the vernacular form.

Thus they have asymmetrical system:

Production
Perception

Standard	Nonstandard
Nonstandard	

This tendency to process the semantic components directly can be seen even more dramatically in responses to sentences with embedded questions; for example:

MODEL:
I asked Alvin if he knows how to play basketball.

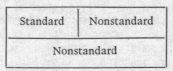

BOOT:

I ax Alvin do he know how to play basketball.

MONEY:

I ax Alvin if – do he know how to play basketball.

MODEL:

I asked Alvin whether he knows how to play basketball.

LARRY F:

1. I axt Alvin does he know how to play basketball.
2. I axt Alvin does he know how to play basketball.

Here the difference between the words used in the model sentence and in the repetition is striking. Again, there is a failure to pass the test. But it is also true that these boys understand the standard sentence, and translate it with extraordinary speed into the NNE form, which is here the regular Southern colloquial form. This form retains the inverted order to signal the underlying meaning of the question, instead of the complementizer *if* or *whether* which standard English uses for this purpose. Thus Boot, Money and Larry perceive the deep structure of the model sentence (Figure 1). The complementizers *if* or *whether* are not required to express this underlying meaning. They are merely two of the formal options which one dialect selects to signal the embedded question. The colloquial Southern form utilizes a different device – preserving the order of the direct question. To say that this dialect lacks the means for logical expression is to confuse logic with surface detail.

To pass the repetition test, Boot and the others have to learn to listen to surface detail. They do not need a new logic; they need practice in paying attention to the explicit form of any utterance rather than its meaning. Careful attention to surface features is a temporary skill needed for language learning – and neglected thereafter by competent speakers. Nothing more than this is involved in the language training in the Bereiter and Engelmann program, or in most methods of teaching English. There is of course nothing wrong with learning to be explicit. As we have seen, that is one of the main advantages of standard English at its best; but it is important that we recognize what is actually taking place, and what teachers are in fact trying to do.

I doubt if we can teach people to be logical, though we can teach them to recognize the logic that they use. Piaget has shown us that in middle-class children logic develops much more slowly than grammar, and that we cannot expect four-year-olds to have mastered the conservation of quantity, let alone syllogistic reasoning.

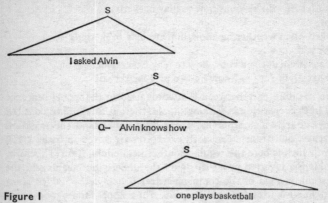

Figure 1

The problems working-class children may have in handling logical operations are not to be blamed on the structure of their language. There is nothing in the vernacular which will interfere with the development of logical thought, for the logic of standard English cannot be distinguished from the logic of any other dialect of English by any test that we can find.

What's wrong with being wrong?

If there is a failure of logic involved here, it is surely in the approach of the verbal deprivation theorists, rather than in the mental abilities of the children concerned. We can isolate six distinct steps in the reasoning which has led to programs such as those of Deutsch, Bereiter and Engelmann:

1. The lower-class child's verbal response to a formal and threatening situation is used to demonstrate his lack of verbal capacity, or verbal deficit.

2. This verbal deficit is declared to be a major cause of the lower-class child's poor performance in school.

3. Since middle-class children do better in school, middle-class speech habits are seen to be necessary for learning.

4. Class and ethnic differences in grammatical form are equated with differences in the capacity for logical analysis.

5. Teaching the child to mimic certain formal speech patterns used by middle-class teachers is seen as teaching him to think logically.

6. Children who learn these formal speech patterns are then said to be thinking logically and it is predicted that they will do much better in reading and arithmetic in the years to follow.

In the previous sections of this paper, I have tried to show that these propositions are wrong, concentrating on (1), (4) and (5). Proposition (3) is the primary logical fallacy which illicitly identifies a form of speech as the *cause* of middle-class achievement in school. Proposition (6) is the one which is most easily shown to be wrong in fact, as we will note below.

However, it is not too naïve to ask, 'What is wrong with being wrong?' There is no competing educational theory which is being dismantled by this program; and there does not seem to be any great harm in having children repeat *This is not a box* for twenty minutes a day. We have already conceded that NNE children need help in analysing language into its surface components, and in being more explicit. But there are serious and damaging consequences of the verbal deprivation theory which may be considered under two headings: theoretical bias, and consequences of failure.

Theoretical bias

It is widely recognized that the teacher's attitude towards the child is an important factor in his success or failure. The work of Rosenthal and Jacobson (1968) on self-fulfilling prophecies shows that the progress of children in the early grades can be dramatically affected by a single random labelling of certain children as 'intellectual bloomers'. When the everyday language of Negro children is stigmatized as 'not a language at all' and 'not possessing the means for logical thought', the effect of such a labelling is repeated many times during each day of the school year. Every time that a child uses a form of NNE without the copula or with negative concord, he will be labelling himself for the teacher's benefit as 'illogical', as a 'nonconceptual thinker'. Bereiter and Engelmann, Deutsch and Jensen are giving teachers a ready-made, theoretical basis for the prejudice they already feel against the lower-class Negro child and his language. When they hear him say *I don't want none* or *They mine*, they will be hearing through the bias provided by the verbal deprivation theory: not an English dialect different from theirs, but the primitive mentality of the savage mind.

But what if the teacher succeeds in training the child to use the new language consistently? The verbal deprivation theory holds that this will lead to a whole chain of successes in school, and that the child will be drawn away from the vernacular culture into the middle-class world. Undoubtedly this will happen with a few isolated individuals, just as it happens in every school system today, for a few children. But we are concerned not with the few but the many, and for the majority of Negro children the distance between them and the school is bound to widen under this approach.

Proponents of the deficit theory have a strange view of social organization outside of the classroom; they see the attraction of the peer group as a 'substitute' for success and gratification normally provided by the school. For example, Whiteman and Deutsch (1968, pp. 86–7) introduce their account of the deprivation hypothesis with an eye-witness account of a child who accidentally dropped his school notebook into a puddle of water and walked away without picking it up: 'A policeman who had been standing nearby walked over to the puddle and stared at the notebook with some degree of disbelief.' The child's alienation from school is explained as the result of his coming to school without the 'verbal, conceptual, attentional and learning skills requisite to school success'. The authors see the child as 'suffering from feelings of inferiority because he is failing; . . . he withdraws or becomes hostile, finding gratification elsewhere, such as in his peer group'.

To view the peer group as a mere substitute for school shows an extraordinary lack of knowledge of adolescent culture. In our studies in south-central Harlem we have seen the reverse situation: the children who are rejected by the peer group are quite likely to succeed in school. In middle-class suburban areas, many children do fail in school because of their personal deficiencies; in ghetto areas, it is the healthy, vigorous, popular child with normal intelligence who cannot read and fails all along the line. It is not necessary to document here the influence of the peer group upon the behavior of youth in our society; but we may note that somewhere between the time that children first learn to talk and puberty, their language is restructured to fit the rules used by their peer group. From a linguistic viewpoint, the peer group is certainly a more powerful influence than the family (for example, Gans, 1962). Less directly, the pressures of peer-group activity are also felt within the school. Many children particularly those who are not doing well in school, show a sudden sharp down-turn in the fourth and fifth grades, and children in the ghetto schools are no exception. It is at the same age, at nine or ten years old, that the influence of the vernacular peer group becomes predominant (see Wilmott, 1966). Instead of dealing with isolated individuals, the school is then dealing with children who are integrated into groups of their own, with rewards and value systems which oppose those of the school. Those who know the sociolinguistic situation cannot doubt that reaction against the Bereiter–Engelmann approach in later years will be even more violent on the part of the students involved, and that the rejection of the school system will be even more categorical.

The essential fallacy of the verbal-deprivation theory lies in tracing the educational failure of the child to his personal deficiencies. At present, these deficiencies are said to be caused by his home environment. It is traditional to explain a child's failure in school by his inadequacy; but when failure reaches such massive proportions, it seems to us necessary to look at the social and cultural obstacles to learning, and the inability of the school to adjust to the social situation. Operation Headstart is designed to repair the child, rather than the school; to the extent that it is based upon this inverted logic, it is bound to fail.

Consequences of failure

The second area in which the verbal deprivation theory is doing serious harm to our educational system is in the consequences of this failure, and the reaction to it. As failures are reported of Operation Headstart, the interpretations which we receive will be from the same educational psychologists who designed this program. The fault will be found not in the data, the theory, nor in the methods used, but rather in the children who have failed to respond to the opportunities offered to them. When Negro children fail to show the significant advance which the deprivation theory predicts, it will be further proof of the profound gulf which separates their mental processes from those of civilized, middle-class mankind.

A sense of the 'failure' of Operation Headstart is already in the air. Some prominent figures in the program are reacting to this situation by saying that intervention did not take place early enough. Caldwell (1967, p. 16) notes that:

... the research literature of the last decade dealing with social-class differences has made abundantly clear that all parents are not qualified to provide even the basic essentials of physical and psychological care to their children.

The deficit theory now begins to focus on the 'long-standing patterns of parental deficit' which fill the literature. 'There is, perhaps unfortunately,' writes Caldwell (1967, p. 17), 'no literacy test for motherhood.' Failing such eugenic measures, she has proposed 'educationally oriented day care for culturally deprived children between six months and three years of age'. The children are returned home each evening to 'maintain primary emotional relationships with their own families', but during the day they are removed to 'hopefully prevent the deceleration in rate of development which seems to occur in many deprived children around the age of two to three years'.

There are others who feel that even the best of the intervention programs, such as those of Bereiter and Engelmann, will not help the Negro child no matter when they are applied – that we are faced once again with the 'inevitable hypothesis' of the genetic inferiority of the Negro people. Many readers of this paper are undoubtedly familiar with the paper of Arthur Jensen in the *Harvard Educational Review* (1969) which received immediate and widespread publicity. Jensen (p. 3) begins with the following quotation from the United States Commission on Civil Rights (1967) as evidence of the failure of compensatory education:

The fact remains, however, that none of the programs appear to have raised significantly the achievement of participating pupils, as a group, within the period evaluated by the Commission (p. 138).

Jensen believes that the verbal deprivation theorists with whom he had been associated – Deutsch, Whiteman, Katz, Bereiter – have been given every opportunity to prove their case – and have failed. This opinion is part of the argument which leads him to the overall conclusion that 'the preponderance of the evidence is ... less consistent with a strictly environmental hypothesis than with the genetic hypothesis'; that racism, or the belief in the genetic inferiority of Negroes, is a correct view in the light of the present evidence.

Jensen argues that the middle-class white population is differentiated from the working-class white and Negro population in the ability for 'cognitive or conceptual learning', which Jensen calls Level II intelligence as against mere 'associative learning' or Level I intelligence:

Certain neural structures must also be available for Level II abilities to develop, and these are conceived of as being different from the neural structures underlying Level I. The genetic factors involved in each of these types of ability are presumed to have become differentially distributed in the population as a function of social class, since Level II has been most important for scholastic performance under the traditional methods of instruction (Jensen, 1969, p. 114).

Jensen found, for example, that one group of middle-class children were helped by their concept-forming ability to recall twenty familiar objects that could be classified into four categories: animals, furniture, clothing, or foods. Lower-class Negro children did just as well as middle-class children with a miscellaneous set, but showed no improvement with objects that could be so categorized.

The research of the educational psychologists cited here is presented in formal and objective style, and is widely received as impartial scientific evidence. Jensen's paper has already been reported by Joseph Alsop and William F. Buckley Jr (*New York Post*, 20 March 1969) as 'massive, apparently authoritative ...'. It is not my intention to examine these materials in detail; but it is important to realize that we are dealing with special pleading by those who have a strong personal commitment. Jensen is concerned with class differences in cognitive style and verbal learning. His earlier papers incorporated the cultural deprivation theory which he now rejects as a basic explanation.[15] Jensen (1968, p. 167) classified the Negro

15. In Deutsch, *et al.* (1968), Jensen expounds the verbal deprivation theory in considerable detail. For example: 'During this "labelling" period

children who fail in school as 'slow-learners' and 'mentally-re-
tarded', and urged that we find out how much their retardation is
due to environmental factors and how much is due to 'more basic
biological factors'. (Jensen, 1968, p. 167). His conviction that the
problem must be located in the child leads him to accept and reprint
some truly extraordinary data. To support the genetic hypothesis
Jensen (1969, p. 83) cites the following percentage estimates by
Heber (1968) of the racial distribution of mental retardation (based
upon IQs below seventy-five) in the general population:[16]

Table 1
Estimated prevalence of children with IQs below 75

SES	White	Negro
1	0·5	3·1
2	0·8	14·5
3	2·1	22·8
4	3·1	37·8
5	7·8	42·9

These estimates, that almost half of lower-class Negro children are
mentally retarded, could be accepted only by someone who has no
knowledge of the children or the community. If he had wished to,

some very important social-class differences may exert their effects on
verbal learning. Lower-class parents engage in relatively little of this
naming or "labelling" play with their children ... That words are
discrete labels for things seems to be better known by the middle-class
child entering first grade than by the lower-class child. Much of this
knowledge is gained in the parent-child interaction, as when the parent
looks at a picture book with the child ...' (p. 119).

16. Heber's studies of eighty-eight Negro mothers in Milwaukee are
cited frequently throughout Jensen's paper. The estimates in this table
are not given in relation to a particular Milwaukee sample, but for the
general United States population. Heber's study was specifically designed
to cover an area of Milwaukee which was known to contain a large
concentration of retarded children, Negro and white, and he has stated
that his findings were 'grossly misinterpreted' by Jensen (*Milwaukee Sen-
tinel,* 11 June 1969).

Jensen could easily have checked this against the records of any school in any urban ghetto area. Taking IQ tests at their face value, there is no correspondence between these figures and the communities we know. For example, among seventy-five boys we worked with in central Harlem who would fall into status categories 4 or 5, there were only three with IQs below seventy-five: one spoke very little English, one could barely see, and the third was emotionally disturbed. When the second was retested, he scored ninety-one, and the third retested at eighty-seven.[17] There are of course hundreds of realistic reports available to Jensen: he simply selected one which would strengthen his case for the genetic inferiority of Negro children.

The frequent use of tables and statistics by educational psychologists serves to give outside readers the impression that this field is a science and that the opinions of the authors should be given the same attention and respect that we give to the conclusions of physicists or chemists. But careful examination of the input data will often show that there is no direct relationship between the conclusions and the evidence (in Jensen's case, between IQ Tests in a specially selected district of Milwaukee and intelligence of lower-class Negro children). Furthermore, the operations performed upon the data frequently carry us very far from the common-sense experience which is our only safeguard against conclusions heavily weighted by the author's theory. As another example we may take some of the evidence presented by Whiteman and Deutsch for the cultural hypothesis. The core of Deutsch's environmental explanation of low school performance is the Deprivation Index – a numerical scale based on six dichotomized variables. One variable is 'the educational aspirational level of the parent for the child'. Most people would agree that a parent who did not care if a child finished high school would be a disadvantageous factor in the child's educational career. In dichotomizing this variable Deutsch was faced with the fact that the educational aspiration of Negro parents is in fact very high – higher than for the white population, as he shows in

17. The IQ scores given here are from group rather than individual tests and must therefore not be weighted heavily: the scores are from the Pintner-Cunningham test, usually given in the first grade in New York City schools in the 1950s.

other papers.[18] In order to fit this data into the Deprivation Index, he therefore set the cutting point for the deprived group as 'college or less' (Whiteman and Deutsch, 1968, p. 100). Thus if a Negro child's father says that he wants his son to go all the way through college, the child will fall into the 'deprived' class on this variable. In order to receive the two points given to the 'less deprived' on the index, it would be necessary for the child's parent to insist on graduate school or medical school! This decision is never discussed by the authors: it simply stands as a *fait accompli* in the tables. Readers of this literature who are not committed to one point of view would be wise to look as carefully as possible at the original data which lies behind each statement and check the conclusions against their own knowledge of the community and people being described.

No one can doubt that the inadequacy of Operation Headstart and of the verbal deprivation hypothesis has now become a crucial issue in our society.[19] The controversy which has arisen over Jensen's article typically assumes that programs such as Bereiter and Engelmann's have tested and measured the verbal capacity of the ghetto child. The cultural sociolinguistic obstacles to this intervention program are not considered; and the argument proceeds upon the data provided by the large, friendly interviewers that we have seen at work in the extracts given above.

18. Table 15.1 in Deutsch, *et al.* (1967, p. 312, section C), shows that some degree of college training was desired by 96, 97 and 100 per cent of Negro parents in Class levels I, II and III respectively. The corresponding figures for whites were 79, 95 and 97 per cent. In an earlier version of this paper, this discussion could be interpreted as implying that Whiteman and Deutsch had used data in the same way as Jensen to rate the Negro group as low as possible. As they point out [personal communication], the inclusion of this item in the Deprivation Index had the opposite effect and it could easily have been omitted if that had been their intention. They also argue that they had sound statistical grounds for dichotomizing as they did. The criticism which I intended to make is that there is something drastically wrong with operations which produce definitions of deprivation such as the one cited here. It should of course be noted that Whiteman and Deutsch have strongly opposed Jensen's genetic hypothesis and vigorously criticized his logic and data.

19. The negative report of the Westinghouse Learning Corporation and Ohio University on Operation Headstart was published in the *New York*

The linguistic view

Linguists are in an excellent position to demonstrate the fallacies of the verbal-deprivation theory. All linguists agree that nonstandard dialects are highly structured systems. They do not see these dialects as accumulations of errors caused by the failure of their speakers to master standard English. When linguists hear Negro children saying *He crazy* or *Her my friend*, they do not hear a primitive language. Nor do they believe that the speech of working-class people is merely a form of emotional expression, incapable of expressing logical thought.

All linguists who work with NNE recognize that it is a separate system, closely related to standard English but set apart from the surrounding white dialects by a number of persistent and systematic differences. Differences in analysis by various linguists in recent years are the inevitable products of differing theoretical approaches and perspectives as we explore these dialect patterns by different routes – differences which are rapidly diminishing as we exchange our findings. For example, Stewart differs with me on how deeply the invariant *be* of *She be always messin' around* is integrated into the semantics of the copula system with *am, is, are,* and so on. The position and meaning of *have . . . ed* in NNE is very unclear, and there are a variety of positions on this point. But the grammatical features involved are not the fundamental predicators of the logical system. They are optional ways of contrasting, foregrounding, emphasizing, or deleting elements of the underlying sentence. There are a few semantic features of NNE grammar which may be unique to this system. But the semantic features we are talking about here are items such as 'habitual', 'general', 'intensive'. These linguistic

---

Times (on 13 April 1969). This evidence for the failure of the program was widely publicized and it seems likely that the report's discouraging conclusions will be used by conservative Congressmen as a weapon against any kind of expenditure for disadvantaged children, especially Negroes. The two hypotheses mentioned to account for this failure is that the impact of Headstart is lost through poor teaching later on, and more recently, that poor children have been so badly damaged in infancy by their lower-class environment that Headstart cannot make much difference. The third 'inevitable' hypothesis of Jensen is not reported here.

markers are essentially *points of view* – different ways of looking at the same events, and they do not determine the truth values of propositions upon which all speakers of English agree.

The great majority of the differences between NNE and standard English do not even represent such subtle semantic features as those, but rather extensions and restrictions of certain formal rules and different choices of redundant elements. For example, standard English uses two signals to express the progressive, *be* and *-ing*, while NNE often drops the former. Standard English signals the third person in the present by the subject noun phrase and by a third singular *-s*; NNE does not have this second redundant feature. On the other hand, NNE uses redundant negative elements in negative concord, in possessives like *mines*, uses *or either* where standard English uses a simple *or*, and so on.

When linguists say that NNE is a system, we mean that it differs from other dialects in regular and rule-governed ways, so that it has equivalent ways of expressing the same logical content. When we say that it is a separate subsystem, we mean that there are compensating sets of rules which combine in different ways to preserve the distinctions found in other dialects. Thus, as noted above, NNE does not use the *if* or *whether* complementizer in embedded questions, but the meaning is preserved by the formal device of reversing the order of subject and auxiliary.

Linguists therefore speak with a single voice in condemning Bereiter's view that the vernacular can be disregarded. I exchanged views on this matter with all of the participants in the Twentieth Annual Georgetown Round Table where this paper was first presented, and their responses were in complete agreement in rejecting the verbal deprivation theory and its misapprehension of the nature of language. The other papers in the report (Alatis, 1970) of that conference testified to the strength of the linguistic view in this area. It was William Stewart who first pointed out that Negro English should be studied as a coherent system, and in this all of us follow his lead. Dialectologists like Raven McDavid, Albert Marckwardt and Roger Shuy have been working for years against the notion that vernacular dialects are inferior and illogical means of communication. Linguists now agree that teachers must know as much as possible about Negro nonstandard English as a communicative system.

The exact nature and relative importance of the structural differences between NNE and standard English are not in question here. It is agreed that the teacher must approach the teaching of the standard through a knowledge of the child's own system. The methods used in teaching English as a foreign language are recommended, not to declare that NNE is a foreign language, but to underline the importance of studying the native dialect as a coherent system for communication. This is in fact the method that should be applied in any English class.

Linguists are also in an excellent position to assess Jensen's claim that the middle-class white population is superior to the working-class and Negro populations in the distribution of Level II, or conceptual, intelligence. The notion that large numbers of children have no capacity for conceptual thinking would inevitably mean that they speak a primitive language, for even the simplest linguistic rules we discussed above involve conceptual operations more complex than those used in the experiment Jensen cites. Let us consider what is involved in the use of the general English rule that incorporates the negative with the first indefinite. To learn and use this rule, one must first identify the class of indefinites involved – *any*, *one*, *ever*, which are formally quite diverse. How is this done? These indefinites share a number of common properties which can be expressed as the concepts 'indefinite', 'hypothetical', and 'nonpartitive'. One might argue that these indefinites are learned as a simple list, by association learning. But this is only one of the many syntactic rules involving indefinites – rules known to every speaker of English, which could not be learned except by an understanding of their common, abstract properties. For example, everyone knows, unconsciously, that *anyone* cannot be used with preterite verbs or progressives. One does not say, *Anyone went to the party* or *Anyone is going to the party*. The rule which operates here is sensitive to the property [+ hypothetical] of the indefinites. Whenever the proposition is not inconsistent with this feature, *anyone* can be used. Everyone knows, therefore, that one can say *Anyone who was anyone went to the party* or *If anyone went to the party* . . . or *Before anyone went to the party* . . . . There is another property of *anyone* which is grasped unconsciously by all native speakers of English; it is [+ distributive]. Thus if we need one more man for a game of bridge or basketball, and there is a crowd outside, we ask *Do any of you want to play?* not *Do some of you want to play?* In both cases, we are considering a plurality, but with *any*, we consider them one at a time, or distributively.

What are we then to make of Jensen's contention that Level I thinkers cannot make use of the concept *animal* to group together a miscellaneous set of toy animals? It is one thing to say that someone is not in the habit of using a certain skill. But to say that his failure to use it is genetically determined implies dramatic consequences for other forms of behavior, which are not found in experience. The knowledge of what people must do in order to learn language makes Jensen's theories seem more and more distant from the realities of human behaviour. Like Bereiter and Engelmann, Jensen is handicapped by his ignorance of the most basic facts about human language and the people who speak it.

There is no reason to believe that any nonstandard vernacular is in itself an obstacle to learning. The chief problem is ignorance of language on the part of all concerned. Our job as linguists is to remedy this ignorance; but Bereiter and Engelmann want to reinforce it and justify it. Teachers are now being told to ignore the language of Negro children as unworthy of attention and useless for learning. They are being taught to hear every natural utterance of the child as evidence of his mental inferiority. As linguists we are unanimous in condemning this view as bad observation, bad theory and bad practice.

That educational psychology should be strongly influenced by a theory so false to the facts of language is unfortunate; but that children should be the victims of this ignorance is intolerable. It may seem that the fallacies of the verbal-deprivation theory are so obvious that they are hardly worth exposing. I have tried to show that such exposure is an important job for us to undertake. If linguists can contribute some of their available knowledge and energy toward this end, we will have done a great deal to justify the support that society has given to basic research in our field.

References

ALATIS, J. (ed.) (1970), *Georgetown Monographs in Language and Linguistics*, no. 22, Georgetown University Press.

BEREITER, C., and ENGELMANN, S. (1966), *Teaching Disadvantaged Children in the Pre-school*, Prentice-Hall.

BEREITER, C., ENGELMANN, S., OSBORN, J., and REIDFORD, P. A. (1966), 'An academically oriented pre-school for culturally deprived children', in F. Hechinger (ed.), *Pre-school Education Today*, Doubleday.

BERNSTEIN, B. (1966), 'Elaborated and restricted codes: their social origins and some consequences', in A. G. Smith (ed.), *Communication and Culture*, Holt Rinehart & Winston.

BLUM, A. (1970), 'The sociology of mental illness', in J. Douglas (ed.), *Deviance and Respectability*, Basic Books.

CALDWELL, B. M. (1967), 'What is the optimal learning environment for the young child', *Amer. J. Orthopsychiatry*, vol. 27, pp. 8–21.

CHOMSKY, N. (1965), *Aspects of the Theory of Syntax*, MIT Press.

COLEMAN, J. S., *et al.* (1966), *Equality of Educational Opportunity*, US Office of Education.

DEUTSCH, M., *et al.* (1967), *The Disadvantaged Child*, Basic Books.

DEUTSCH, M., KATZ, I., and JENSEN, A. R. (eds.) (1968), *Social Class, Race, and Psychological Development*, Holt, Rinehart & Winston.

GANS, H. (1962), *The Urban Villagers*, Free Press.

HEBER, R. (1968), 'Research on education and habilitation of the mentally retarded', paper read at Conference on Sociocultural Aspects of Mental Retardation, Peabody College, Nashville, Tennessee.

JENSEN, A. R. (1968), 'Social class and verbal learning', in M. Deutsch, *et al.* (eds.), *Social Class, Race, and Psychological Development*, Holt, Rinehart & Winston.

JENSEN, A. R. (1969), 'How much can we boost IQ and scholastic achievement', *Harvard Educational Review*, vol. 39, pp. 1–123.

LABOV, W. (1966), 'On the grammaticality of everyday speech', paper presented at the annual meeting of the Linguistic Society of America, December.

LABOV, W. (1967), 'Some sources of reading problems for Negro speakers of nonstandard English', in A. Frazier (ed.), *New Directions in Elementary English*, National Council of Teachers of English. Reprinted in Baratz, J. C., and Shuy, R. W. (eds.) (1969), *Teaching Black Children to Read*, Center for Applied Linguistics.

LABOV, W. (1968), 'Negative attraction and negative concord in four English dialects', paper presented at the annual meeting of the Linguistic Society of America, December.

LABOV, W. (1969), 'Contraction, deletion, and inherent variability of the English copula', *Language*, vol. 45, pp. 715–62.

LABOV, W., COHEN, P., and ROBINS, C. (1965), *A Preliminary study of the Structure of English used by Negro and Puerto Rican Speakers in New York City*, final report, US Office of Education Cooperative Research Project No. 3091.

LABOV, W., COHEN, P., ROBINS, C., and LEWIS, J. (1968), *A Study of the Nonstandard English of Negro and Puerto Rican Speakers in New York City*, final report, US Office of Education Cooperative Research Project No. 3288.

LABOV, W., and ROBINS, C. (1969), 'A note on the relation of reading failure to peer-group status in the urban ghetto', *Teacher's College Record*, vol. 70, pp. 396–405.

LANGER, T. S., and MICHAELS, S. T. (1963), *Life Stress and Mental Health*, Free Press.

ROSENTHAL, R., and JACOBSON, L. (1968), 'Self-fulfilling prophecies in the classroom: teachers' expectations as unintended determinants of pupils' intellectual competence', in M. Deutsch, *et al.* (eds.), *Social Class, Race and Psychological Development*, Holt, Reinhart & Winston.

UNITED STATES COMMISSION OF CIVIL RIGHTS (1967), *Racial Isolation in the Public Schools*, vol. 1, US Government Printing Office

WHITEMAN, M., and DEUTSCH, M. (1968), 'Social disadvantage as related to intellective and language development', in M. Deutsch, *et al.* (eds.), *Social Class, Race and Psychological Development*, Holt, Rinehart & Winston.

WILMOTT, P. (1966), *Adolescent Boys of East London*, Routledge & Kegan Paul.

2 Jane Torrey
Illiteracy in the Ghetto

Jane W. Torrey, 'Illiteracy in the Ghetto', *Harvard Educational Review*, vol. 40, no. 2, May 1970, pp. 253–9.

For those learning to read, the implications of dialect differences can affect two quite different aspects of language. First, the differences between the Afro-American and standard dialects – in their phonological, grammatical and semantic structures – might lead to confusion and misunderstanding, complicating the already difficult reading process. Second, the cultural and personal functions of language and language differences might affect the social relations between a child and his school in such a way as to block effective learning. It is the thesis of this paper that the functional aspects of language have more serious implications for illiteracy than the structural ones. These functional aspects are closely connected with the conditions of life that keep people out of schools and the conditions of schools that keep people from learning to read in spite of ostensible efforts to teach them.

Although standard English serves as the medium of instruction in reading and other subjects and is the only dialect accepted as 'correct' in the dominant society, the deviations of many black children from the standard forms cannot be regarded as errors. These so-called 'errors' actually conform to discernible grammatical rules, different from those of the standard language, but no less systematic. Furthermore, the patterns of black children's grammar that strike the standard English-speaking teacher as incomplete, illogical or linguistically retarded actually conform closely to rules of adult language spoken in the ghetto environment. The following quotes from children in Harlem illustrate patterns that have been interpreted as showing that such children are 'poorly languaged'.

We at Jane house.
Jane makin' me a cow.
It look like you don' brush your teeth.

While these sentences may appear incomplete or incorrect to standard speakers, the rules of Afro-American English permit the deletion of the words 'is' and 'are' in many contexts. The possessive 's' is also optional and the third person singular of present tense verbs has no distinctive 's' ending. All of these seemingly careless omissions are in fact quite consistent grammatical usages, which are increasingly being interpreted as differences in dialect rather than as deficiencies of language development (Labov, 1969).

On the surface it might seem that structural differences between dialects would be important considerations in teaching speakers of Afro-American to read. Since all or nearly all of the reading materials they meet are in standard English, their situation would be something like that of Spanish-speaking children trying to learn to read English before they could speak it very well. Since the Afro-American phonology involves reduction or deletion of many terminal consonants and modification of the pattern of standard vowel differentiation, there would seem to be special obstacles for the black child in learning phoneme–grapheme correspondences. Many consonants correspond to no audible sounds in his speech, and different vowel letters are used for sounds that are the same to him.

However, the difference in phonology between standard English and black English is not directly relevant to reading. All children who learn to read English have to break a fairly complex code of sound–spelling relationships. The fact that the correspondences are different for speakers of Afro-American does not in itself prove that they are more difficult than for standard speakers.

I have reported elsewhere (Torrey, 1969a) on a five-year-old self-taught reader who could both recognize and spell correctly words that he did not pronounce in a way comprehensible to a speaker of standard English. His Afro-American sound system had no discernible effect on his reading or writing even though he had discovered how to read and write for himself without any instruction or guidance. Similarly children in England or Boston have no particular trouble in learning words that end in 'r' despite the fact that they hardly ever realize these 'r's as such in their speech. These considerations make it seem doubtful that instruction in standard English pronunciation would have any material effect on the ability of black children to learn how to read.

Grammatical differences between the two dialects might also be expected to create problems. However, if we examine specific grammatical differences, we find very few that are likely to lead to misunderstanding. For example, the third person singular present tense verb inflection of standard English, missing in Afro-American, is regarded as one of the most serious problems because it results in many 'errors of subject–verb agreement' in black children's writing. However, it is very difficult to find sentences in standard English that could actually be misunderstood because of failure to attend to this inflection. Number is nearly always signalled by a noun inflection also, so that the verb inflection is entirely redundant. It is possible, but quite difficult, to invent sentences where meaning is dependent upon the verb ending alone. 'The deer runs' would be a case, since only the 's' of 'runs' tells how many deer. However, there are few such nouns in English. People normally attend to the noun as a signal of number, and even speakers of standard English have some trouble using a verb ending as a clue.

There is empirical evidence to suggest that a speaker who uses Afro-American forms often understands the standard forms perfectly well. Labov (Labov, *et al.*, 1968) asked teenage boys to repeat sentences that were presented orally. These boys commonly 'translated' some standard forms into Afro-American as though they were not aware of any difference. For example, *I asked Alvin if he knows how to play basketball* was rendered as *I ax Alvin do he know how to play basketball*. The latter form has the same meaning as the original, showing that the speaker understood the standard version even though he was unable to produce it himself. My own research (Torrey, 1969) has shown that many second-graders in the same area where Labov's subjects lived make this same translation. However, they read the standard forms aloud without changing them.

Another dialect difference is in the possessive inflection. Black children would often say *That's Peter doggie*, when the doggie belongs to Peter. Usually this omission produces no ambiguity, but in the few situations where it does, the children in the second grade seemed to understand the distinctive meaning of the 's'. I asked them to choose between two pictures representing *The man teacher* (a man standing before a class) and *The man's teacher* (a woman teaching with a man in the class). Many could select the latter picture for *The man's teacher* and name the two pictures correctly in standard English even though they themselves did not spontaneously use the possessive 's' in conversation. The same was true with other dialect differences for these children.

From the above evidence it seems unlikely that the failure of many urban children to progress in reading is primarily due to structural differences between their dialect and school English. A passive understanding of standard dialect should suffice for purposes of learning to read, even if a given child never learns to use the standard forms in speech.

Turning from the structural properties of language to its functions, we can roughly distinguish two classes of functions, the intellectual and the social. The intellectual functions include communicating information between people as well as using language as a tool of thought within an individual. It has been supposed by Bernstein (1961) and others that some dialects spoken by members of lower socio-economic classes are intrinsically less adequate for educational purposes than middle-class dialects. However, there has been very little specification of the forms in the substandard dialects that might be inappropriate for intellectual expression and very little evidence that substandard speakers differ from standard speakers in the quality or subtlety of their thought. If there is such a difference favoring standard grammar, the burden of proof is upon those who maintain it exists. Such proof has yet to be presented. Labov (1969) argues cogently that clear expression, logical thought and artistic subtlety are as characteristic of 'lower-class' language as of academese, perhaps more so. In the absence of convincing evidence that any intellectual differences are inherent in language, I would argue that we should look at the social functions of language for possible explanations of the failure of urban schools to teach all black children to read.

Groups and societies could not exist without languages to link their members together. The language of a group is also the medium of its culture, an integral part of its characteristic style of expression and thought. Language and mannerisms of speech are not just passively adopted from the social milieu. People use them as means of expressing themselves and signifying their membership in a community. Language also signals to other people whether a person is likely to become a friend, what his attitudes are and what his social status is.

Speakers of different dialects belong to different subgroups in the larger society, and they usually can identify each other by language alone. Some dialects, such as those associated with regions, may carry no particular status or evaluative significance. Others belong to subgroups of recognized high or low status. The characteristic culture, manners, style and language of the black American have been intimately associated in the minds of black and white alike with his historical status. White America has made it necessary for a black man to divest himself of these cultural traits including dialect in order to change his status or find a secure place in the dominant white society. The schools have regarded it as their prime obligation to stamp out all possible manifestations of black culture and language, assuming that only when that was accomplished could an individual reap the benefits of his education and ability. To the extent they believed that imposing white language and manners was necessary for social advancement, teachers have accepted the acculturating function that was assigned to schools in the handling of foreign immigrants.

My thesis is that the main impact of Afro-American dialect on education has not been its structural differences from standard English, nor its relative intrinsic usefulness as a medium of thought, but its function as a low-status stigma and its association with a rejected culture. The attitudes of teachers toward this dialect and of dialect speakers toward the teachers' language have affected the social relationships of children with the schools in such a way as to make education of many children almost impossible. Black children of rural southern background have entered the urban schools to find that nearly everything they said was branded as 'wrong'. In order to be 'right' they had to adopt forms that seemed alien even when they were able to learn how to use them. Their own spontaneous products were punished and treated as worthless, including the only language they knew really well. Because of this, they were almost forced to regard themselves and their society as bad, ugly or even sinful.

Children in the lower grades commonly accept a teacher as a kind of substitute mother. Teachers make use of this attitude in motivating and teaching. However, no such mother–child relationship can be established with someone who cannot accept the other person and his ways as legitimate. The black child is more likely to become alienated from the teacher and from the culture the teacher represents, including reading, than he is to conform to strange and unfriendly ways. The differences in language and culture become a basis of hostility and rejection of the whole educational process. Indeed, one might speculate that the evolution of an elaborate secret language among blacks has been essential to their survival – that the highly symbolic, metaphorical references used by blacks constitute a defense against the alien culture.

The relationship between black child and white-dominated school parallels the pattern of racial polarization in society and is being increasingly incorporated into the larger struggle. This is not to say that all the black–white division in society and school can be attributed to linguistic differences alone. Illiteracy that occurs in urban America today is not a direct result of language differences, but language is one of the cultural differences that have played a key role in the failure of schools to reach black children.

In other words, one could not claim that schools are imposing an alien language, because there is adequate evidence that the structural differences are minor. But within the social context, minor differences in structure can take on enough symbolic importance to be construed by black children and teachers alike as alien and therefore threatening. Changing the attitudes of teachers toward black English and the attitudes of black children toward standard English will not in itself solve the problem of urban education, but it will almost certainly have to be part of any considerable improvement in school effectiveness. Consideration of the personal and social functions of language is vitally important for deciding when, how and in what spirit to introduce second dialect learning.

The idea that Afro-American English is a legitimate 'language' in its own right has many possible implications for education. The initial response of many educators has been that efforts to teach standard English might make use of the new techniques of foreign language teaching. However, several basic implications should be considered first. One is that the teaching of standard English should not have the purpose of 'stamping out' the native dialect. Standard English would be a second language, or rather, a second dialect, to be available alongside the native one for special purposes such as school and contact with the standard-speaking community. People would still use Afro-American English in their own community and the school would not have to stigmatize it any more than it should condemn the use of Spanish.

Other basic questions raised by this view of Afro-American include, first, whether a command of the standard language is really necessary for educational purposes at all; second, whether in higher education and in the society at large there should be a more flexible interpretation of 'correctness' in spoken and written English; and, finally, whether the Afro-American language and the culture associated with it are not in themselves worthy objects of study in the school curriculum. Should not the grammar of Afro-American be taught just as the grammar of Spanish should for Spanish-speaking children? Should not the folklore and style of that medium be given the same respect as other forms of folk art?

It would be unrealistic to talk of changing the attitudes of grade school teachers toward linguistic variation without at the same time proposing other changes in the whole educational and occupational systems. It would be dishonest to raise children in an atmosphere of cultural and linguistic tolerance in the early grades if they found at higher levels of school and in the job market that their own language was regarded as inferior and that only the traditional literature and science were treated as worthwhile knowledge. The academic world in general must broaden its cultural base beyond those subjects, methods and media that have been traditional in schools and universities, or else they will continue to discriminate in fact against the 'other' cultures and languages of the nation. We should stop asking schools and colleges to be the instruments of melting down our cultural variety and originality, as the Spanish conquerors melted down the metallurgical art of the Incas into square gold bars of value on the Euro-American market. LeRoi Jones looked around the city and saw a lot of 'square gray buildings' built by 'square grays'. Many of those buildings were schools turning out illiterates because they could not adjust to all the different shapes of their task. Our traditional cultural and linguistic imperialism has been self-defeating not only because it has failed to acculturate its more divergent elements, but also because it has prevented our nation as a whole from appreciating the true richness of its diverse heritage.

References

BERNSTEIN, B. (1961), 'Social structure, language and learning'. *Educational Research*, no. 3, 163–76.

LABOV, W. (1969), 'The logic of nonstandard English', *Georgetown Monograph Series on Languages and Linguistics*, no. 22.

LABOV, W., COHEN, P., ROBINS, C., and LEWIS, J. (1968), *A Study of the Nonstandard English of Negro and Puerto Rican Speakers in New York City*, final report, US Office of Education Cooperative Research Project No. 3288.

TORREY, J. W. (1969), 'Teaching standard English to speakers of other dialects', paper prepared for the Second International Congress of Applied Linguistics, September.

TORREY, J. W. (1969a), 'Learning to read without a teacher: a case study', *Elementary English*, no. 46, pp. 550–56.

3 Estelle Fuchs
How Teachers Learn to Help Children Fail

Estelle Fuchs, 'How teachers learn to help children fail', *Transactions,*
September 1968, pp. 45–9.

Ideally, public schools exist to educate the child. But a high percentage of pupils fail as early as the fifth or sixth grade, especially in
the urban slums. For many children, the educational process bogs
down at a time when it has barely begun. Now, educators and social
scientists have proposed a number of theories to explain this high
rate of failure among slum-school children. One of them is that the
slum-school system's tacit belief that social conditions outside the
school make such failures inevitable *does* make such failures inevitable.

How this expectation of failure affects the instruction of lower-
class children and becomes a self-fulfilling prophecy is suggested in
data collected by Hunter College's Project TRUE (Teacher Resources
for Urban Education), a study that focused on the experiences of
fourteen fledgling teachers in New York's inner-city elementary
schools. As part of the study, several new teachers tape-recorded
accounts of their first-semester teaching experiences in 'special service' schools – schools that invariably had high Negro or Puerto
Rican enrollments, retarded reading levels among the students and
constant discipline problems.

The following excerpts from one teacher's account show how the
slum school gradually instills, in even the best-intentioned teacher,
the prevailing rationale for its own failure: the idea that in the slum,
it is the child and the family who fail, but never the school.

26 October

Mrs Jones, the sixth-grade teacher, and I were discussing reading
problems. I said, 'I wonder about my children. They don't seem too

slow; they seem average. Some of them even seem to be above average. I can't understand how they can grow up to be fifth- and sixth-graders and still be reading on the second-grade level. It seems absolutely amazing.'

Mrs Jones (an experienced teacher) explained about the environmental problems that these children have. 'Some of them never see a newspaper. Some of them have never been on the subway. The parents are so busy having parties and things that they have no time for their children. They can't even take them to a museum or anything. It's very important that the teacher stress books.'

Mrs Jones tells her class, 'If anyone asks you what you want for Christmas, you can say you want a book.' She told me that she had a 6-1 class last year, and it was absolutely amazing how many children had never even seen a newspaper. They can't read Spanish either. So she said that the educational problem lies with the parents. They are the ones that have to be educated.

It's just a shame that the children suffer. This problem will take an awful lot to straighten it out. I guess it won't take one day or even a year; it will take time.

14 December

Here I am, a first-grade teacher. I get a great thrill out of these children being able to read but I often wonder, 'Am I teaching them how to read or are they just stringing along sight words that they know?' I never had a course in college for teaching phonetics to children. In this school we have had conferences about it, but I really wish that one of the reading teachers would come in and specifically show me how to go about teaching phonetics. I have never gotten a course like this and it is a difficult thing, especially when there is a language barrier and words are quite strange to these children who can't speak English. How can they read English? We have a great responsibility on our shoulders and the teachers should take these things seriously.

4 January

Something very, very important and different has happened to me in my school. It all happened the last week before the vacation on

Tuesday. Mr Frost, our principal, came over to me and asked if I would be willing to take over a second-grade class starting after the vacation. Well, I looked at him and I said, 'Why?'

He told me briefly that the registers in the school have dropped and according to the board of education the school must lose a teacher. Apparently he was getting rid of a second-grade teacher and he wanted to combine two of the first-grade classes. The registers on the first grade were the lowest in the school, I believe. Anyway, he told me that he was going to all the afternoon first-grade teachers asking if any of them would be willing to change in the middle of the term. He said he thought perhaps someone would really want it and, instead of his just delegating a person, it would be better if he asked each one individually.

I was torn between many factors. I enjoyed my class very, very much and I enjoyed teaching the first grade. But because I was teaching afternoon session (our school runs on two different sessions), I was left out of many of the goings-on within the school as my hours were different and it also sort of conflicted with my home responsibilities. Well, with these two points in mind, I really felt that I would rather stay with my class than switch over in the middle of term.

But he explained further that some of the classes would not remain the same because there would be many changes made. So, being the type of person that I am, I felt that, even though I did want to stay with my class and the children and the first grade, if something had to be done in the school, there was no way of stopping it and I might as well do it. I explained to Mr Frost that even though I wouldn't want to change in the middle – after all it would be a whole new experience, two classes of children would be suffering by the change – but if it had to be done I would be willing to take on the new responsibility.

With that, Mr Frost said, 'Thank you', and said he would go around to the other teachers to see if anyone really wanted to change. Well, already I felt that it was going to be me, but I wasn't sure.

A little later on in the day I was taking my class to recess, and we were lining up in the hall. I spoke to Miss Lane, another teacher, and she said that he had also spoken to her. At that point Mr Frost came over and told me that he was sorry but that I had been the one elected. Well, I said that I hoped that I would be able to do a good job, and that was that.

From that point on, there was an awful lot of talk in the school. Everybody was talking about it, at least, everyone who knew something about the matter. So all the afternoon first-grade teachers and all the morning first-grade teachers knew, and many of the new teachers (those that I came into the school with), and apparently there was a lot of business going on that I can't begin to describe because I don't know how the whole thing started in the first place. However, from the office I did find out that it wasn't Mr Frost's fault or anything that the second-grade teacher was going to be dismissed. It was a directive from higher up that stated he would lose a teacher. How he chose this particular teacher to let go I really can't say. I understand that they really didn't get along too well and neither of them were too happy in the school working together.

Everything went so quickly and everybody was talking to me. Mrs Parsons spoke to me. She is my assistant principal. She was supervisor of the first grade and she will be in charge of the second grade also. I was told that I would have to take over the new class on 2 January, the first day that we return from the vacation. I really felt terrible about my children, but it was something that had to be done and I did it.

Thursday, Mr Frost talked to the other afternoon teachers and myself. He referred to me as the hero and he said, 'Now it is your turn to be heroes also.' He asked the afternoon first-grade teachers if they would be willing to have their registers become higher by having my twenty-seven children split up among the four remaining afternoon classes, or did they think he should have them split up among all the first-grade classes, some of which met in the morning.

He was straightforward, saying that he didn't think it would be a good idea for the children to be split up among all the first-grade teachers. I agreed with him. He felt that it would be trying on the parents and on the children to have a whole new schedule worked out. After all, if you're used to going to school from 12 to 4, coming to school from 7.30 to 11 is quite a difference. It would be very, very hard on the parents. Especially in this neighborhood where sometimes they have a few children in the same grade, a few in different grades. So I agreed with Mr Frost. The other teachers didn't seem too happy about the idea, but they said they would go along with it.

Mr Frost and Mrs Parsons worked out a plan whereby the 1-1 class register would go up to thirty-five which is generally what a 1-1 class has. The 1-3 class register would go up to thirty-two or thirty-three. And so forth down the line, 1-5 (my class) would be erased. The teachers didn't think it was so bad then, but we all did have added responsibilities.

Mr Frost then added that if we had any children in our classes that we felt did not belong, this was our chance to have them changed, since there would be many interclass transfers in order to make more homogeneous classes. So we all had to sit down and think 'Who belongs? Who doesn't belong?' I, of course, had to decide, where twenty-seven children would belong.

Class is divided

I went through my class and divided them into groups to the best of my ability. In the 1-1 class, I put Joseph R., who scored the highest on the reading-readiness test. As a result of his score and his work in class, I felt Joseph did belong in the 1-1 class. Lydia A., who I believe is a very smart girl and who wasn't really working as well as she could in my class, I felt belonged in the 1-1 class. Lydia scored second highest on the reading-readiness test. In the 1-1 class, I also put Anita R. Anita is a bit older than the rest of the children but she has caught on most beautifully to most phases of school work even though she just came to the United States last March. Also, she scored the same as Lydia on the reading-readiness test.

Then I decided that I would put Robert M. in the 1-1 class. I felt strongly that Robert was by far the best child in my class. Robert did every bit of the work ever assigned. He caught on very, very quickly to all phases of work besides doing his work well, quickly, efficiently and neatly. Even though on reading-readiness he only scored in the fiftieth percentile, I felt he really stood out and I also felt that once you're in a '1' class, unless you really don't belong, you have a better chance. The '1' class is really the only class that you would term a 'good' class. So those four children I recommended for the 1-1 class.

Then I went down the line and for the 1-3 class, I picked nine children, really good children who, on the whole, listened and did their work. Most of them scored in the fiftieth and fortieth percentile on reading-readiness, and they were coping with school problems very, very well. In the 1-7 class, I put the slower children and in the 1-9 class, of course, which is Mrs Gould's, I put all the children that really weren't doing well in school work at all. First, Alberto S. Alberto is still not able to write his name. Then I put Beatrice L., Stella S., Pedro D. and several others, who really were not working well, in the 1-9 class.

I know that the other teachers do have a big job before them because whichever class these children are placed in will not have been doing exactly the same work. The children either have much to catch up on or they might review some of the work, and the teachers will have to be patient either way. I really don't think anyone will have serious discipline problems, except perhaps in the 1-1 class where Lydia and Anita have been placed.

Telling the children

The time came when I had to tell the children that I would not be their teacher anymore. Well, as young as they are, I think that many of them caught on immediately, and before I could say anything, faces were very, very long and the children were mumbling, 'But I wanted you for a teacher.'

That was all I needed! I felt even worse than I felt when I found out that I wouldn't be with them anymore. So I continued talking and I told them that it's just something that happens and that I would still be in the school and maybe next year they would get me when they go to the second grade. I told them that I would miss them all, that they would have a lot of fun in their new classes, and they would learn a lot. And, of course, I said, 'You know all the other teachers. Some of you will get Mrs Lewis. Some will get Miss Lane, some will get Miss Taylor, and some will get Mrs Gould.'

To my astonishment Anita kept saying over and over, 'But I want you for a teacher. But I want you for a teacher.'

I looked around the room. Most of the children were sitting there with very, very long faces. Joseph C. was sitting there with the longest face you could imagine, Robert G. said he didn't want another teacher, and all of a sudden Joseph started crying and just didn't stop. He cried all the way out into the hall when we got dressed to go home. I spoke to him softly and said, 'Joseph, wouldn't you like Miss Lane for a teacher?' She was standing right near me, and finally he stopped crying.

I said goodbye to them and that I would see them all. And that was the end of my class . . .

Good schools. Poor schools. What is a good school? Is a good school one that is in a good neighborhood, that has middle-class children? Is a poor school one in a depressed area where you have Negro and Puerto Rican children? These are common terms that people refer to all the time. They hear your school is on Wolf Street – 'Oh, you must be in a bad school.'

I don't really think that that is what a good or a bad school is. I think a good school is a school that is well run, has a good administration, has people that work together well, has good discipline and where the children are able to learn and also, of course, where there are numerous facilities for the children and the teachers. In my estimation a poor or a bad school would be one in which the administration and the teachers do not work together, are not working in the best interests of the children, and where learning is not going on. Also, a poor school is one where you don't have proper facilities. I am not acquainted with many of the public schools, and I really can't say that the ones that I know are better or worse.

I believe my school is a pretty good school. It isn't in the best neighborhood. There are many, many problems in my school but on the whole I think that the teachers and the administration work together and I do believe that they are doing the best they can with the problems that are around.

You have to remember that in a school such as ours the children are not as ready and willing to learn as in schools in middle-class neighborhoods.

Discussion

When a new teacher enters the classroom, she must learn the behavior, attitudes and skills required in the new situation. Much of this learning is conscious. Some of it is not. What is significant is that, while on the job, the teacher is socialized to her new role – she is integrated into the society of the school, and learns the values, beliefs and attitudes that govern its functioning.

The saga of class 1-5 shows the subtle ways in which one new teacher is socialized to her job. In just a few months, she accepts the demands of the school organization and its prevailing rationale for student failure.

The new teacher of class 1-5 in a slum school begins her career with a warm, friendly attitude toward her students. She respects and admires their abilities and is troubled by what the future holds for them: by the sixth grade in her school, educational failure is very common.

Very early in her teaching career, however, a more experienced teacher exposes this new teacher to the belief, widely held, that the children come from inferior backgrounds and that the deficits in their homes – expressed here as lack of newspapers and parental care – prevent educational achievement. That the teachers and the school as an institution contribute to the failure of the children is never even considered as a possible cause. The beginning teacher, in her description of what happens to class 1-5, then provides us with a graphic account of the ways in which this attitude can promote failure.

First, let us examine the actual instruction of the children. Early in her career, this new, very sincere teacher is painfully aware of her own deficiencies. Unsure about her teaching of so fundamental a subject as reading, she raises serious questions about her own effectiveness. As yet, she has not unconsciously accepted the notion that the failure of children stems from gaps in their backgrounds. Although no consensus exists about reading methodology, the teacher tells us that there are serious weaknesses in feedback evaluation – and that she is unable to find out what the children have been taught or what they have really learned.

By the end of the term, all this has changed. By that time, the eventual failure of most of class 1-5 has been virtually assured. And the teacher has come to rationalize this failure in terms of pupil inadequacy.

In the particular case of class 1-5, the cycle of failure begins with a drop in the number of students registered in the school. The principal loses a teacher, which in turn means dissolving a class and subsequently distributing its children among other classes. The principal and the teachers have no control over this event. In the inner-city schools, education budgets, tables of organization and directions from headquarters create conditions beyond the control of the administrators and teachers who are in closest touch with the children.

A drop in pupil registers would seemingly provide the opportunity for a higher adult–pupil ratio and, consequently, more individualized instruction and pedagogical support for both youngsters and teachers. In a suburban school, this is probably what would have occurred. But in this slum school, the register drop leads to the loss of a teacher, larger classes and – perhaps most important – increased time spent by the administrator and his staff on the mechanics of administration rather than on the supervision of instruction. (Why *this* particular teacher is released is unclear, though her substitutes status and low rank in the staff hierarchy probably contribute to her release.) As a result many classes are disrupted, several first-grade class registers grow larger, time for instruction is lost, and concern is felt by teachers and pupils alike.

An even more significant clue to the possible eventual failure of the children is described in poignant detail – when the teacher tells how the youngsters in her class are to be distributed among the other first-grade classes. Educators now know that children mature at different rates; that they have different rates of learning readiness; and the developmental differences between boys and girls are relevant to learning. To forecast the educational outcome of youngsters at this early stage of their development, without due provision for these normal growth variations, is a travesty of the educational process. Yet here, in the first half of the first grade, a relatively inexperienced young teacher, herself keenly aware of her own deficiencies as an educator, is placed in the position of literally deciding the educational future of her charges.

A few are selected for success: 'I felt that once you're in a "1" class, unless you really don't belong, you have a better chance. The "1" class is really the only class that you would term a "good" class.' Several children are placed in a class labelled 'slow'. And the remaining youngsters are relegated to a state of limbo, a middle range that does not carry the hope of providing a 'better chance'.

Early tracking of children's futures

Thus, before these youngsters have completed a full four months of schooling, their educational futures have been 'tracked': all through the grades, the labels of their class placement will follow them, accompanied by teacher attitudes about their abilities. Some youngsters are selected very early for success, others written off as slow. Because differential teaching occurs and helps to widen the gap between children, the opportunity to move from one category to another is limited. In addition, the children too become aware of the labels placed upon them. And their pattern for achievement in later years is influenced by their feelings of success or failure in early school experiences.

The teacher, as she reflects upon what a 'good' or a 'bad' school is, continues to include how well the children learn as a significant criterion, together with good relations between staff and administration. But the children in her school do not achieve very well academically, so when describing her school as 'good', she stresses the good relations between the administration and the teachers. The fact that the children do not learn does not seem so important now: 'the children are not as ready and willing to learn as in schools in middle-class neighborhoods'.

How well our teacher has internalized the attitude that deficits of the children themselves explain their failure in school! How normal she now considers the administrative upheavals and their effects upon teachers and children! How perfectly ordinary she considers the 'tracking' of youngsters so early in their school years!

The teacher of class 1-5 has been socialized by the school to accept its structure and values. Despite her sincerity and warmth and obvious concern for the children, this teacher is not likely to change the forecast of failure for most of these children – because she has come to accept the very structural and attitudinal factors that make failure nearly certain. In addition, with all her good intentions, she has come to operate as an agent determining the life chances of the children in her class — by distributing them among the ranked classes on the grade.

This teacher came to her job with very positive impulses. She thought highly of her youngsters and was disturbed that, with what appeared to be good potential, there was so much failure in the school in the upper grades. She looked inward for ways in which she might improve her efforts to forestall retardation. She was not repelled by the neighborhood in which she worked. There is every indication that she had the potential to become a very effective teacher of disadvantaged youngsters.

Her good impulses, however, were not enough. This young teacher, unarmed with the strength that understanding the social processes involved might have given her and having little power within the school hierarchy, was socialized by the attitudes of those around her, by the administration and by the availability of a suitable rationale to explain her and the school's failure to fulfill their ideal roles. As a result she came to accept traditional slum-school attitudes toward the children — and traditional attitudes toward school organization as the way things have to be. This teacher is a pleasant, flexible, cooperative young woman to have on one's staff. But she has learned to behave and think in a way that perpetuates a process by which disadvantaged children continue to be disadvantaged.

The organizational structure of the large inner-city school and the attitudes of the administrators and teachers within it clearly affect the development of the children attending. No theory proposed to explain the academic failure of poor and minority-group children can ignore the impact of the actual school experience and the context in which it occurs.

4 Neil Postman
The Politics of Reading[1]

Neil Postman, 'The politics of reading', *Harvard Educational Review*, vol. 40, no. 2, May 1970, pp. 244–52.

Teachers of reading comprise a most sinister political group, whose continued presence and strength are more a cause for alarm than celebration. I offer this thought as a defensible proposition, all the more worthy of consideration because so few people will take it seriously.

My argument rests on a fundamental and, I think, unassailable assumption about education: namely, that all educational practices are profoundly political in the sense that they are designed to produce one sort of human being rather than another – which is to say, an educational system always proceeds from some model of what a human being *ought* to be like. In the broadest sense, a political ideology is a conglomerate of systems for promoting certain modes of thinking and behavior. And there is no system I can think of that more directly tries to do this than the schools. There is not one thing that is done to, for, with or against a student in school that is not rooted in a political bias, ideology or notion. This includes everything from the arrangement of seats in a classroom, to the rituals practiced in the auditorium, to the textbooks used in lessons, to the dress required of both teachers and students, to the tests given, to the subjects that are taught and, most emphatically, to the intellectual skills that are promoted. And what is called reading, it seems to me, just about heads the list. For to teach reading, or even to promote vigorously the teaching of reading, is to take a definite political position on how people should behave and on what they ought to value. Now, teachers, I have found, respond in one of three ways to such an assertion. Some of them deny it. Some of them concede it

1. An earlier version of this article was presented as the keynote address at the Lehigh University Reading Conference, 24 January 1970.

but without guilt or defensiveness of any kind. And some of them don't know what it means. I want to address myself to the latter, because in responding to them I can include all the arguments I would use in dealing with the others.

In asserting that the teaching of reading is essentially a political enterprise, the most obvious question i am asking is, 'What is reading good for?' When I ask this question of reading teachers, I am supplied with a wide range of answers. Those who take the low ground will usually say that skill in reading is necessary in order for a youngster to do well in school. The elementary teacher is preparing the youngster for the junior high teacher, who prepares him for the senior high teacher, who, in turn, prepares him for the college teacher, and so on. Now, this answer is true but hardly satisfactory. In fact, it amounts to a description of the *rules* of the school game but says nothing about the purpose of these rules. So, when teachers are pushed a little further, they sometimes answer that the school system, at all levels, makes reading skill a precondition to success because unless one can read well, he is denied access to gainful and interesting employment as an adult. This answer raises at least a half-dozen political questions, the most interesting of which is whether or not one's childhood education ought to be concerned with one's future employment. I am aware that most people take it as axiomatic that the schooling process should prepare youth for a tranquil entry into our economy, but this is a political view that I think deserves some challenge. For instance, when one considers that the second most common cause of death among adolescents in the US is suicide, or that more people are hospitalized for mental illness than all other illnesses combined, or that one out of every twenty-two murders in the United States is committed by a parent against his own child, or that more than half of all high school students have already taken habit-forming, hallucinogenic or potentially addictive narcotics, or that by the end of this year, there will be more than one-million school drop-outs around, one can easily prepare a case which insists that the schooling process be designed for purposes other than vocational training. If it is legitimate at all for schools to claim a concern for the adult life of students, then why not pervasive and compulsory programs in mental health, sex, or marriage and the family? Besides, the number of jobs that require reading skill much beyond what teachers call a 'fifth-grade level' is probably quite small and scarcely justifies the massive, compulsory, unrelenting reading programs that characterize most schools.

But most reading teachers would probably deny that their major purpose is to prepare students to satisfy far-off vocational requirements. Instead, they would take the high ground and insist that the basic purpose of reading instruction is to open the student's mind to the wonders and riches of the written word, to give him access to great fiction and poetry, to permit him to function as an informed citizen, to have him experience the sheer pleasure of reading. Now, this is a satisfactory answer indeed but, in my opinion, it is almost totally untrue.

And to the extent that it is true, it is true in a way quite different from anything one might expect. For instance, it is probably true that in a highly complex society, one cannot be governed unless he can read forms, regulations, notices, catalogues, road signs, and the like. Thus, some minimal reading skill is necessary if you are to be a 'good citizen', but 'good citizen' here means one who can follow the instructions of those who govern him. If you cannot read, you cannot be an obedient citizen. You are also a good citizen if you are an enthusiastic consumer. And so, some minimal reading competence is required if you are going to develop a keen interest in all the products that it is necessary for you to buy. If you do not read, you will be a relatively poor market. In order to be a good and loyal citizen, it is also necessary for you to believe in the myths and superstitions of your society. Therefore, a certain minimal reading skill is needed so that you can learn what these are, or have them reinforced. Imagine what would happen in a school if a Social Studies text were introduced that described the growth of American civilization as being characterized by four major developments:

1. insurrection against a legally constituted government, in order to achieve a political identity;
2. genocide against the indigenous population in order to get land;
3. keeping human beings as slaves, in order to achieve an economic base;
4. the importation of 'coolie' labor, in order to build the railroads.

Whether this view of American history is true or not is beside the point. It is at least as true or false as the conventional view *and* it would scarcely be allowed to appear unchallenged in a school-book intended for youth. What I am saying here is that an important function of the teaching of reading is to make students accessible to political and historical myth. It is entirely possible that the main reason middle-class whites are so concerned to get lower-class blacks to read is that blacks will remain relatively inaccessible to standard-brand beliefs unless and until they are minimally literate. It just may be too dangerous, politically, for any substantial minority of our population *not* to believe that our flags are sacred, our history is noble, our government is representative, our laws are just and our institutions are viable. A reading public is a responsible public, by which is meant that it believes most or all of these superstitions, and which is probably why we still have literacy tests for voting.

One of the standard beliefs about the reading process is that it is more or less neutral. Reading, the argument goes, is just a skill. What people read is their own business, and the reading teacher merely helps to increase a student's options. If one wants to read about America, one may read DeToqueville or the *Daily News*; if one wants to read literature, one may go to Melville or Jacqueline Susann. In theory, this argument is compelling. In practice, it is pure romantic nonsense. The *New York Daily News* is the most widely read newspaper in America. Most of our students will go to the grave not having read, of their own choosing, a paragraph of DeToqueville or Thoreau or John Stuart Mill or, if you exclude the Gettysburg Address, even Abraham Lincoln. As between Jacqueline Susann and Herman Melville — well, the less said, the better. To put it bluntly, among every hundred students who learn to read, my guess is that no more than one will employ the process toward any of the lofty goals which are customarily held before us. The rest will use the process to increase their knowledge of trivia, to maintain themselves at a relatively low level of emotional maturity, and to keep themselves simplistically uninformed about the social and political turmoil around them.

Now, there are teachers who feel that, even if what I say is true, the point is nonetheless irrelevant. After all, they say, the world is not perfect. If people do not have enough time to read deeply, if people do not have sensibilities refined enough to read great literature, if people do not have interests broad enough to be stimulated by the unfamiliar, the fault is not in our symbols, but in ourselves. But there is a point of view that proposes that the 'fault', in fact, *does* lie in our symbols. Marshall McLuhan is saying that each medium of communication contains a unique metaphysic – that each medium makes special kinds of claims on our senses, and therefore, on our behavior. McLuhan himself tells us that he is by no means the first person to have noticed this. Socrates took a very dim view of the written word, on the grounds that it diminishes man's capacity to memorize, and that it forces one to follow an argument rather than to participate in it. He also objected to the fact that once something has been written down, it may easily come to the attention of persons for whom it was not intended. One can well imagine what Socrates would think about wire-tapping and other electronic bugging devices. St Ambrose, a prolific book-writer and reader, once complained to St Jerome, another prolific writer and reader, that whatever else its virtues, reading was the most anti-social behavior yet devised by man. Other people have made observations about the effects of communications media on the psychology of a culture, but it is quite remarkable how little has been said about this subject. Most criticism of print, or any other medium, has dealt with the content of the medium; and it is only in recent years that we have begun to understand that each medium, *by its very structure*, makes us do things with our bodies, our senses and our minds that in the long run are probably more important than any other messages communicated by the medium.

Now that it is coming to an end, we are just beginning to wonder about the powerful biases forced upon us by the Age of the Printed Word. McLuhan is telling us that print is a 'hot' medium, by which he means that it induces passivity and anesthetizes almost all our senses except the visual. He is also telling us that electronic media, like the LP record and television, are re-ordering our entire sensorium, restoring some of our sleeping senses, and, in the process, making all of us seek more active participation in life. I think McLuhan is wrong in connecting the *causes* of passivity and activity so directly to the structure of media. I find it sufficient to say that whenever a new medium — a new communications technology — enters a culture, *no matter what its structure*, it gives us a new way of experiencing the world, and consequently releases tremendous energies and causes people to seek new ways of organizing their institutions. When Gutenberg announced that he could manufacture books, as he put it, 'without the help of reeds, stylus or pen but by wondrous agreement, proportion and harmony of punches and types', he could scarcely imagine that he was about to become the most important political and social revolutionary of the Second Millenium. And yet, that is what happened. Four hundred and fifty years ago, the printed word, far from being a medium that induced passivity, generated cataclysmic change. From the time Martin Luther posted his theses in 1517, the printing press disseminated the most controversial, inflammatory and wrenching ideas imaginable. The Protestant Reformation would probably not have occurred if not for the printing press. The development of both capitalism and nationalism were obviously linked to the printing press. So were new literary forms, such as the novel and the essay. So were new conceptions of education, such as written examinations. And, of course, so was the concept of scientific methodology, whose ground rules were established by Descartes in his *Discourse on Reason*. Even today in recently illiterate cultures, such as Cuba, print is a medium capable of generating intense involvement, radicalism, artistic innovation and institutional upheaval. But in those countries where the printed word has been pre-eminent for over 400 years, print retains very few of these capabilities. Print is not dead, it's just old — and old technologies do not generate new patterns of behavior. For us, print is the technology of convention. We have accommodated our senses to it. We have routinized and even ritualized our responses to it. We have devoted our institutions, which are now venerable, to its service. By maintaining the printed word as the keystone of education, we are therefore opting for political and social stasis.

It is 126 years since Professor Morse transmitted a message electronically for the first time in the history of the planet. Surely it is not too soon for educators to give serious thought to the message he sent: 'What hath God wrought?' We are very far from knowing the answers to that question, but we do know that electronic media have released unprecedented energies. It's worth saying that the gurus of the peace movement – Bob Dylan, Pete Seeger, Joan Baez, Phil Ochs, for instance – were known to their constituency mostly as voices on LP records. It's worth saying that Viet Nam, being our first television war, is also the most unpopular war in our history. It's worth saying that Lyndon Johnson was the first president ever to have resigned because of a 'credibility gap'. It's worth saying that it is now commonplace for post-TV college sophomores to usurp the authority of college presidents and for young parish priests to instruct their bishops in the ways of *both* man and God. And it's also worth saying that black people, after 350 years of bondage, want their freedom – now. Post-television blacks are, indeed, our true *now* generation.

Electronic media are predictably working to unloose disruptive social and political ideas, along with new forms of sensibility and expression. Whether this is being achieved by the structure of the media, or by their content, or by some combination of both, we cannot be sure. But like Gutenberg's infernal machine of 450 years ago, the electric plug is causing all hell to break loose. Meanwhile, the schools are still pushing the old technology; and, in fact, pushing it with almost hysterical vigor. Everyone's going to learn to read, even if we have to kill them to do it. It is as if the schools were the last bastion of the old culture, and if it has to go, why let's take as many down with us as we can.

For instance, the schools are still the principal source of the idea that literacy is equated with intelligence. Why, the schools even promote the idea that *spelling* is related to intelligence! Of course, if any of this were true, reading teachers would be the smartest people around. One doesn't mean to be unkind, but if that indeed is the case, no one has noticed it. In any event, it is an outrage that children who do not read well, or at all, are treated as if they are stupid. It is also masochistic, since the number of non-readers will obviously continue to increase and, thereby, the schools will condemn themselves, by their own definition of intelligence, to an increasing number of stupid children. In this way, we will soon have remedial reading-readiness classes, along with remedial classes for those not yet ready for their remedial reading-readiness class.

The schools are also still promoting the idea that literacy is the richest source of aesthetic experience. This, in the face of the fact that kids are spending a billion dollars a year to buy LP records and see films. The schools are still promoting the idea that the main source of wisdom is to be found in libraries, from which most schools, incidentally, carefully exclude the most interesting books. The schools are still promoting the idea that the non-literate person is somehow not fully human, an idea that will surely endear us to the non-literate peoples of the world. (It is similar to the idea that salvation is obtainable only through Christianity – which is to say, it is untrue, bigoted, reactionary and based on untenable premises, to boot.)

Worst of all, the schools are using these ideas to keep non-conforming youth – blacks, the politically disaffected and the economically disadvantaged, among others – in their place. By taking this tack, the schools have become a major force for political conservatism at a time when everything else in the culture screams for rapid re-orientation and change.

What would happen if our schools took the dramatic political step of trying to make the new technology the keystone of education? The thought will seem less romantic if you remember that the start of the Third Millenium is only thirty-one years away. No one knows, of course, what would happen, but I'd like to make a few guesses. In the first place, the physical environment would be entirely different from what it is now. The school would look something like an electric circus – arranged to accommodate TV cameras and monitors, film projectors, computers, audio and video tape machines, radio and photographic and stereophonic equipment. As he is now provided with textbooks, each student would be provided with his own still-camera, 8 mm. camera and tape cassette. The school library would contain books, of course, but at least as many films, records, video-tapes, audio-tapes and computer programs. The major effort of the school would be to assist students in achieving what has been called 'multi-media literacy'. Therefore, speaking, film-making, picture-taking, televising, computer-programming, listening, perhaps even music playing, drawing and dancing would be completely acceptable means of expressing intellectual interest and competence. They would certainly be given weight at least equal to reading and writing.

Since intelligence would be defined in a new way, a student's ability to create an idea would be at least as important as his ability to classify and remember the ideas of others. New evaluation procedures would come into being, and standardized tests – the final, desperate refuge of the print-bound bureaucrat – would disappear. Entirely new methods of instruction would evolve. In fact, schools might abandon the notion of teacher-instruction altogether. Whatever disciplines lent themselves to packaged, lineal and segmented presentation would be offered through a computerized and individualized program. And students could choose from a wide variety of such programs whatever they wished to learn about. This means, among other things, that teachers would have to stop acting like teachers and find something useful to do, like, for instance, helping young people to resolve some of their more wrenching emotional problems.

In fact, a school that put electric circuitry at its center would have to be prepared for some serious damage to all of its bureaucratic and hierarchical arrangements. Keep in mind that hierarchies derive their authority from the notion of unequal access to information. Those at the top have access to more information than those at the bottom. That is in fact why they are at the top and the others at the bottom. But today those who are at the bottom of the school hierarchy, namely, the students, have access to at least as much information about most subjects as those at the top. At present, the only way those at the top can maintain control over them is by carefully discriminating against what the students know – that is, by labelling what the students know as unimportant. But suppose cinematography was made a 'major' subject instead of English literature? Suppose chemotherapy was made a 'major' subject? or space technology? or ecology? or mass communication? or popular music? or photography? or race relations? or urban life? Even an elementary school might then find itself in a situation where the faculty were at the bottom and its students at the top. Certainly, it would be hard to know who are the teachers and who the learners.

And then perhaps a school would become a place where *everybody*, including the adults, is trying to learn something. Such a school would obviously be problem-centered, *and* future-centered, *and* change-centered; and, as such, would be an instrument of cultural and political radicalism. In the process we might find that our youth would also learn to read without pain and with a degree of success and economy not presently known.

I want to close on this thought: teachers of reading represent an important political pressure group. They may not agree with me that they are a sinister political group. But I should think that they would want to ask at least a few questions *before* turning to consider the *techniques* of teaching reading. These questions would be: what is reading good for? What is it better or worse than? What are my motives in promoting it? And the ultimate political question of all, 'Whose side am I on?'

5 Margaret Mead
Our Educational Emphases in Primitive Perspective

Margaret Mead, 'Our educational emphases in primitive perspective', *American Journal of Sociology*, vol. 48, 1942–3, pp. 633–9.

In its broadest sense, education is the cultural process, the way in which each newborn human infant, born with a potentiality for learning greater than that of any other mammal, is transformed into a full member of a specific human society, sharing with the other members a specific human culture.[1] From this point of view we can place side by side the newborn child in a modern city and the savage infant born into some primitive South Sea tribe. Both have everything to learn. Both depend for that learning upon the help and example, the care and tutelage, of the elders of their societies. Neither child has any guarantee of growing up to be a full human being should some accident, such as theft by a wolf, interfere with its human education. Despite the tremendous difference in what the New York infant and the New Guinea infant will learn, there is a striking similarity in the whole complicated process by which the child takes on and into itself the culture of those around it. And much profit can be gained by concentrating on these similarities and by setting the procedure of the South Sea mother side by side with the procedure of the New York mother, attempting to understand the common elements in cultural transmission. In such comparisons we can identify the tremendous potentialities of human beings, who are able to learn not only to speak any one of a thousand languages but to adjust to as many different rhythms of maturation, ways of learning, methods of organizing their emotions and of managing their relationships to other human beings.

In this paper, however, I propose to turn away from this order of comparison – which notes the differences between human cultures,

1. This paper is an expression of the approach of the Council on Inter-cultural Relations.

primitive and civilized, only as means of exploring the processes which occur in both types of culture – and to stress instead the ways in which our present behavior, which we bracket under the abstraction 'education', differs from the procedures characteristic of primitive homogeneous communities. I propose to ask, not what there is in common between America in 1941 and South Sea culture which displays in 1941 a Stone Age level of culture, but to ask instead: what are some of the conspicuous differences, and what light do these differences throw upon our understanding of our own conception of education? And, because this is too large and wide a subject, I want to limit myself still further and to ask a question which is appropriate to this symposium: what effects has the mingling of peoples – of different races, different religions and different levels of cultural complexity – had upon our concept of education? When we place our present-day concept against a backdrop of primitive educational procedures and see it as influenced by intermingling of peoples, what do we find?

I once lectured to a group of women – all of them college graduates – alert enough to be taking a fairly advanced adult-education course on 'Primitive Education' delivered from the first point of view. I described in detail the lagoon village of the Manus tribe, the ways in which the parents taught the children to master their environment, to swim, to climb, to handle fire, to paddle a canoe, to judge distances and calculate the strength of materials. I described the tiny canoes which were given to the three-year-olds, the miniature fish spears with which they learned to spear minnows, the way in which small boys learned to caulk their canoes with gum, and how small girls learned to thread shell money into aprons. Interwoven with a discussion of the more fundamental issues, such as the relationship between children and parents and the relationships between younger children and older children, I gave a fairly complete account of the type of adaptive craft behavior which was characteristic of the Manus and the way in which this was learned by each generation of children. At the end of the lecture one woman stood up and asked the first question: 'Didn't they have any vocational training?' Many of the others laughed at the question, and I have often told it myself as a way of getting my audience into a mood which was less rigidly limited by our own phrasing of 'education'. But that woman's question, naïve and crude as it was, epitomized a long series of changes which stand between our idea of education and the processes by which members of a homogeneous and relatively static primitive society transmit their standardized habit patterns to their children.

There are several striking differences between our concept of education today and that of any contemporary primitive society[2]; but perhaps the most important one is the shift from the need for an individual to learn something which everyone agrees he would wish to know, to the will of some individual to teach something which it is not agreed that anyone has any desire to know. Such a shift in emphasis could come only with the breakdown of self-contained and self-respecting cultural homogenity. The Manus or the Arapesh or the Iatmul adults taught their children all that they knew themselves. Sometimes, it is true, there were rifts in the process. A man might die without having communicated some particular piece of ritual knowledge; a good hunter might find no suitable apprentice among his available near kin, so that his skill perished with him. A girl might be so clumsy and stupid that she never learned to weave a mosquito basket that was fit to sell. Miscarriages in the smooth working of the transmission of available skills and knowledge did occur, but they were not sufficient to focus the attention of the group upon the desirability of *teaching* as over against the desirability of *learning*. Even with considerable division of labor and with a custom by which young men learned a special skill not from a father or other specified relative but merely from a master of the art, the master did not go seeking pupils; the pupils and their parents went to seek the master and with proper gifts of fish or octopus or dogs' teeth persuaded him to teach the neophyte. And at this level of human culture even close contact with members of other cultures did not alter the emphasis. Women who spoke another language married into the tribe; it was, of course, very important that they should learn to speak the language of their husbands' people, and so they learned that language as best they could – or failed to learn it. People might compliment them on their facility or laugh at them for their lack of it, but the idea of *assimilatinf* them was absent.

2. This discussion, unless otherwise indicated, is based upon South Sea people only.

Similarly, the spread of special cults or sects among South Sea people, the desire to *join* the sect rather than the need to make converts, was emphasized. New ceremonies did develop. It was necessary that those who had formerly been ignorant of them should learn new songs or new dance-steps, but the onus was again upon the learner. The greater self-centeredness of primitive homogeneous groups (often so self-centered that they divided mankind into two groups – the human beings, i.e., themselves, and the nonhuman beings, other people) preserved them also from the emphasis upon the greater value of one truth over another which is the condition of proselytizing. '*We* (human beings) do it this way and *they* (other people) do it that way.' A lack of a desire to teach *them* our ways guaranteed also that the *we* group had no fear of any proselytizing from the *they* groups. A custom might be imported, bought, obtained by killing the owner, or taken as part of a marriage payment. A custom might be exported for a price or a consideration. But the emphasis lay upon the desire of the importing group to obtain the new skill or song and upon the desire of the exporting group for profit in material terms by the transaction. The idea of conversion, or purposely attempting to alter the ideas and attitudes of other persons, did not occur. One might try to persuade one's brother-in-law to abandon his own group and come and hunt permanently with the tribe into which his sister had married; physical proselytizing there was, just as there was actual import and export of items of culture. But, once the brother-in-law had been persuaded to join a different cultural group, it was his job to learn how to live there; and you might, if you were still afraid he would go back or if you wanted his cooperation in working a two-man fish net, take considerable pains to teach him this or that skill as a bribe. But to bribe another by teaching him one's own skill is a long way from any practice of conversion, although it may be made subsidiary to it.

We have no way of knowing how often in the course of human history the idea of Truth, as a revelation to or possession of some one group (which thereby gained the right to consider itself superior to all those who lacked this revelation), may have appeared. But certain it is that, wherever this notion of hierarchical arrangements of cultural views of experience appears, it has profound effects upon education; and it has enormously influenced our own attitudes toward education. As soon as there is any attitude that one set of cultural beliefs is definitely superior to another, the framework is present for active proselytizing, unless the idea of cultural superiority is joined with some idea of hereditary membership, as it is among the Hindus. (It would indeed be interesting to investigate whether any group which considered itself in possession of the most superior brand of religious or economic truth, and which did not regard its possession as limited by heredity, could preserve the belief in that superiority without proselytizing. It might be found that active proselytizing was the necessary condition for the preservation of the essential belief in one's own revelation.) Thus, with the appearance of religions which held this belief in their own infallible superiority, education becomes a concern of those who teach rather than of those who learn. Attention is directed toward finding neophytes rather than toward finding masters, and adults and children become bracketed together as recipients of conscious missionary effort. This bracketing-together is of great importance; it increases the self-consciousness of the whole educational procedure, and it is quite possible that the whole question of methods and techniques of education is brought most sharply to the fore when it is a completely socialized adult who must be influenced instead of a plastic and receptive child.

With social stratification the possibility of using education as a way of changing status is introduced, and another new component of the educational idea develops. Here the emphasis is still upon the need to learn – on the one hand, in order to alter status and, on the other, to prevent the loss of status by failure to learn. But wherever this possibility enters in there is also a possibility of a new concept of education developing from the relationship between fixed caste and class lines and education. In a static society members of different caste or class groups may have been teaching their children different standards of behavior for many generations without any essential difference between their attitudes toward education and those of less complex societies. To effect a change it is necessary to focus the attention of the members of the society upon the problem, as conditions of cultural contact do focus it. Thus, in present-day Bali, the high castes are sending their daughters to the Dutch schools to be trained as schoolteachers because it is pre-eminently important that learning should be kept in the hands of the high castes and profoundly inappropriate that low-caste teachers should teach high-caste children. They feel this strongly enough to overcome their prejudices against the extent to which such a course takes high-caste women out into the market place.

As soon as the possibility of shift of class position by virtue of a different educational experience becomes articulately recognized, so that individuals seek not only to better their children or to guard them against educational defect but also to see the extension of restriction of educational opportunity as relevant to the whole class structure, another element enters in – the relationship of education to social change. Education becomes a mechanism of change. Public attention, once focused upon this possibility, is easily turned to the converse position of emphasizing education as a means toward preserving the status quo. I argue here for no historical priority in the two positions. But I am inclined to believe that we do not have catechumens taught to say 'to do my duty in that state of life into which it has pleased God to call me' until we have the beginning of movements of individuals away from their birth positions in society. In fact, the whole use of education to defend vested interests and intrenched privilege goes with the recognition that education can be a way of encroaching upon them. Just as the presence of proselytizing religions focuses attention upon means of spreading the truth, upon pedagogy, so the educational implications of social stratification focus attention upon the content of education and lay the groundwork for an articulate interest in the curriculum.

Movements of peoples, colonization and trade also bring education into a different focus. In New Guinea it is not uncommon to 'hear' (i.e., understand without speaking) several languages besides one's own, and many people not only 'hear' but also speak neighboring languages. A head-hunting people like the Mundugumor, who had the custom of giving child hostages to temporary allies among the neighboring peoples, articulately recognized that it was an advantage to have members of the group be well acquainted with the roads, the customs and the language of their neighbors, who would assuredly at some time in any given generation be enemies and objects of attack. Those who took the hostages regarded this increased facility of the Mundugumor as a disadvantage which had to be put up with. But the emphasis remained with the desirability of learning. Today, with the growth of pidgin English as a *lingua franca*, bush natives and young boys are most anxious to learn pidgin. Their neighbors, with whom they could trade and communicate more readily if they knew pidgin, are not interested in teaching them. But the European colonist is interested. He sees his position as an expanding, initiating, changing one; he wants to trade with the natives, to recruit and indenture them to work on plantations. He needs to have them speak a language that he can understand. Accordingly, we have the shift from the native who needs to learn another language in order to understand to the colonist who needs someone else to learn a language so that he, the colonist, may be understood. In the course of teaching natives to speak some *lingua franca*, to handle money, to work copra, etc., the whole focus is on teaching; not, however, on techniques of teaching, in the sense of pedagogy, but upon sanctions for making the native learn. Such usages develop rapidly into compulsory schooling in the language of the colonist or the conqueror, and they result in the school's being seen as an adjunct of the group in power rather than as a privilege for those who learn.

Just as conquest or colonization of already inhabited countries brings up the problems of assimilation, so also mass migrations may accentuate the same problem. This has been true particularly in the United States, where education has been enormously influenced by the articulate need to assimilate the masses of European immigrants, with the resulting phrasing of the public schools as a means for educating other peoples' children. The school ceased to be chiefly a device by which children were taught accumulated knowledge or skills and became a political device for arousing and maintaining national loyalty through inculcating a language and a system of ideas which the pupils did not share with their parents.

It is noteworthy that, in the whole series of educational emphases which I have discussed here as significant components of our present-day concept of 'education', one common element which differentiates the ideas of conversion, assimilation, successful colonization and the relationship between class-caste lines and education from the attitude found in primitive homogeneous societies is the acceptance of discontinuity between parents and children. Primitive education was a process by which continuity was maintained between parents and children, even if the actual teacher was not a parent but a maternal uncle or a shaman. Modern education includes a heavy emphasis upon the function of education to create discontinuities – to turn the child of the peasant into a clerk, of the farmer into a lawyer, of the Italian immigrant into an American, of the illiterate into the literate. And parallel to this emphasis goes the attempt to use education as an extra, special prop for tottering continuities. Parents who are separated from their children by all the gaps in understanding which are a function of our rapidly changing world cling to the expedient of sending their children to the same schools and colleges they attended, counting upon the heavy traditionalism of slow-moving institutions to stem the tide of change. (Thus, while the father builds himself a new house and the mother furnishes it with modern furniture, they both rejoice that back at school, through the happy accident that the school is not well-enough endowed, son will sit at the same desk at which his father sat.) The same attitude is reflected by the stock figure of the member of a rural school board who says, 'What was good enough for me in school is good enough for my children. The three R's, that's enough.'

Another common factor in these modern trends of education is the increasing emphasis upon change rather than upon growth, upon what is done to people rather than upon what people do. This emphasis comes, I believe, from the inclusion of adults as objects of the educational effort – whether the effort comes from missionaries, colonizers, conquerors, Old Americans, or employers of labor. When a child is learning to talk, the miracle of learning is so pressing and conspicuous that the achievement of the teachers is put in the shade. But the displacement, in an adult's speech habits, of his native tongue by the phonetics of some language which he is being bullied or cajoled into learning is often more a matter of triumph for the teacher than of pride for the learner. Changing people's habits, people's ideas, people's language, people's beliefs, people's emotional allegiances, involves a sort of deliberate violence to other people's developed personalities – a violence not to be found in the whole teacher–child relationship, which finds its prototype in the cherishing parent helping the young child to learn those things which are essential to his humanity.

We have been shocked in recent years by the outspoken brutality of the totalitarian states, which set out to inculcate into children's minds a series of new ideas which it was considered politically useful for them to learn. Under the conflicting currents of modern ideologies the idea of *indoctrination* has developed as a way of characterizing the conscious educational aims of any group with whom the speaker is out of sympathy. Attempts to teach children any set of ideas in which one believes have become tainted with suspicion of power and self-interest, until almost all education can be branded and dismissed as one sort of indoctrination or another. The attempt to assimilate, convert, or keep in their places other human beings conceived of as inferior to those who are making the plans has been a boomerang which has distorted our whole educational philosophy; it has shifted the emphasis from one of growth and seeking for knowledge to one of dictation and forced acceptance of clichés and points of view. Thus we see that the presence of one element within our culture – a spurious sense of superiority of one group of human beings over another, which gave the group in power the impetus to force their language, their beliefs and their culture down the throats of the group which was numerically, or economically, or geographically handicapped – has corrupted and distorted the emphases of our free schools.

But there has been another emphasis developing side by side with those which I have been discussing, and that is a belief in the power of education to work miracles – a belief which springs from looking at the other side of the shield. As long as the transmission of culture is an orderly and continuous process, in a slowly changing society, the child speaks the language of his parents; and, although one may marvel that this small human being learns at all, one does not marvel that he learns French or English or Samoan, provided that this be the language of the parents. It took the discontinuity of educational systems, purposive shifts of language and beliefs between parents and children, to catch our imagination and to fashion the great American faith in education as creation rather than transmission, conversion, suppression, assimilation or indoctrination.

Perhaps one of the most basic human ways of saying 'new' is 'something that my parents have never experienced' or, when we speak of our children, 'something I have never experienced'. The drama of discontinuity which has been such a startling feature of modern life, and for which formal education has been regarded in great measure as responsible, suggested to men that perhaps education might be a device for creating a new kind of world by developing a new kind of human being.

Here it is necessary to distinguish sharply between the sort of idea which George Counts expressed in his speech, 'Dare the Schools Build a New Social Order?', and the idea of education as creation of something new. Dr Counts did not mean a new social order in the sense of an order that no man had dreamed of, so much as he meant a very concrete and definite type of society for which he and many others believed they had a blueprint. He was asking whether the teachers would use the schools to produce a different type of socio-economic system. His question was still a power question and partook of all the power ideas which have developed in the long period during which men in power, men with dominating ideas, men with missions, have sought to put their ideas over upon other men. His question would have been phrased more accurately as 'Dare the schools build a different social order?' The schools of America have these hundred years been training children to give allegiance to a way of life that was new to them, not because they were children to whom all ways were new, not because the way of life was itself one that no man had yet dreamed of, but because they were the children of their parents. Whenever one group succeeds in getting power over the schools and teaches within those schools a doctrine foreign to many of those who enter those doors, they are building up, from the standpoint of those students, a different social order. From the standpoint of those in power, they are defending or extending the old; and, from the moment that the teachers had seriously started to put Dr Counts's suggestion into practice, they would have been attempting by every method available to them to extend, in the minds of other people's children, their own picture, already an 'old' idea, of the sort of world they wanted to live in.

It is not this sort of newness of which I speak. But from those who watched learning, those who humbly observed miracles instead of claiming them as the fruits of their strategy or of their superior teaching (propaganda) techniques, there grew up in America a touching belief that it was possible by education to build a new world – a world that no man had yet dreamed and that no man, bred as we had been bred, could dream. They argued that if we can bring up our children to be freer than we have been – freer from anxiety, freer from guilt and fear, freer from economic constraint and the dictates of expediency – to be equipped as we never were equipped, trained to think and enjoy thinking, trained to feel and enjoy feeling, then we shall produce a new kind of human being, one not known upon the earth before. Instead of the single visionary, the depth of whose vision has kept men's souls alive for centuries, we shall develop a whole people bred to the task of seeing with clear imaginative eyes into a future which is hidden from us behind the smoke screen of our defective and irremediable educational handicaps. This belief has often been branded as naïve and simple-minded. The American faith in education, which Clark Wissler lists as one of the dominant American culture traits, has been held up to ridicule many times. In many of its forms it is not only unjustified optimism but arrant nonsense. When small children are sent out by overzealous schoolteachers to engage in active social reforms – believed necessary by their teachers – the whole point of view becomes not only ridiculous but dangerous to the children themselves.

Phrased, however, without any of our blueprints, with an insistence that it is the children themselves who will some day, when they are grown, make blueprints on the basis of their better upbringing, the idea is a bold and beautiful one, an essentially democratic and American idea. Instead of attempting to bind and limit the future and to compromise the inhabitants of the next century by a long process of indoctrination which will make them unable to follow any path but that which we have laid down, it suggests that we devise and practice a system of education which sets the future free. We must concentrate upon teaching our children to walk so steadily that we need not hew too straight and narrow paths for them but can trust them to make new paths through difficulties we never encountered to a future of which we have no inkling today.

When we look for the contributions which contacts of peoples, of peoples of different races and different religions, different levels of culture and different degrees of technological development, have made to education, we find two. On the one hand, the emphasis has shifted from learning to teaching, from the doing to the one who causes it to be done, from spontaneity to coercion, from freedom to power. With this shift has come the development of techniques of power, dry pedagogy, regimentation, indoctrination, manipulation and propaganda. These are but sorry additions to man's armory, and they come from the insult to human life which is perpetuated whenever one human being is regarded as differentially less or more human than another. But, on the other hand, out of the discontinuities and rapid changes which have accompanied these minglings of people has come another invention, one which perhaps would not have been born in any other setting than this one – the belief in education as an instrument for the creation of new human values.

We stand today in a crowded place, where millions of men mill about seeking to go in different directions. It is most uncertain whether the educational invention made by those who emphasized teaching or the educational invention made by those who emphasized learning will survive. But the more rapidly we can erase from our society those discrepancies in position and privilege which tend to perpetuate and strengthen the power and manipulative aspects of education, the more hope we may have that that other invention – the use of education for unknown ends which shall exalt man above his present stature – may survive.

6 Thomas Gladwin
Culture and Logical Process

Thomas Gladwin, 'Culture and logical process', in Ward Goodenough (ed.) (1964), *Explorations in Cultural Anthropology: Essays in Honour of George Peter Murdoch*, McGraw-Hill

In 1936, Gregory Bateson published *Naven* (1958, 2nd edn), an admittedly partial ethnography of the Iatmul of New Guinea. The importance of this book lay in his attempt to formulate some theoretical constructs with respect to psychological process and social dynamics, constructs which would embrace his observations of the Iatmul, and would at the same time be of general validity. One of these, *schizmogenesis*, was developed extensively and ultimately led Bateson into cybernetics and the flourishing field of general systems research. The other really new concept in *Naven*, *eidos*, has never enjoyed the equal development it deserves.

Eidos, in Bateson's terms, is 'a standardization (and expression in cultural behavior) of the cognitive aspects of the personality of individuals' (1958, p. 220). It is complementary to *ethos*, 'the expression of a culturally standardized system of organization of the instincts and emotions of . . . individuals' (1958, p. 118). Early in the history of research in culture and personality, Bateson thus made explicit the necessity for giving to the cognitive aspects of personality a weight and attention equal to that devoted to the emotional.

However, earlier exploratory thinking by Edward Sapir and others on the relationship between culture and personality had been rooted in the concepts of psychoanalysis, a system of theory anchored almost exclusively to the biological and emotional determinants of psychological process. Then, in the year following the publication of *Naven*, Ralph Linton went to Columbia and soon became the dominant figure in a group of anthropologists collaborating with the distinguished analyst, Abram Kardiner. The impact on anthropology of their work was so great that since that time the main stream of research and theoretical development in culture and personality has virtually taken for granted the assumption that its primary data are to be found in the realm of emotion. It is ironic that of all the fields of inquiry into human behavior, anthropology, with its primary emphasis on the regularities of behavior as they are transmitted through culture from one generation to the next, is the one which most consistently ignores the cognitive learning involved in this cultural transmission.

True, the theory of learning formulated by Clark Hull has had considerable vogue in anthropology, but this theory is far more concerned with motivation and reward for learning than it is with the cognitive integrations accomplished in learning. Aside from Hullian theory, attention to the processes of learning and thinking, and to the nature of intelligence, has been minimal in anthropology. Bateson did carry *eidos* one step farther, developing in collaboration with Margaret Mead the concept of *deutero-learning* (Bateson, 1942), referring to learning how to learn or to the content and logical process of learning. This was a useful concept, and although they did not develop it farther, both Bateson and Mead are far more careful than most anthropologists to make explicit the nature of the learning process in the cultures they have described. More recently the emerging field of psycholinguistics and contributions to a few symposia have reflected a growing interest in cognitive categories and processes, but this remains a scattered effort.[1] It is in no way comparable to the numerous but sometimes frustrating endeavors of anthropologists to derive a variety of personality types from common emotional experiences ordered within a Freudian framework.

I became acutely aware of this neglect by anthropologists some six years ago when, in collaboration with Seymour B. Sarason, I undertook a review of research in mental subnormality (Masland, Sarason and Gladwin, 1958). The first question of course was, what is mental normality? – i.e., how do we define intelligence? This is obviously a difficult question, even disregarding cultural differences. Most psychologists in effect define intelligence operationally as being

1. e.g., Symposium on Cognitive Structures, American Anthropological Association, Mexico City, December 1959, at which an earlier version of this paper was presented. See also Tanner and Inhelder (1960) and Gladwin and Sturtevant (1962).

that which intelligence tests measure. People with high IQs are intelligent, and those with low IQs are variously dull, duller or idiots. There has been much soul-searching by psychologists on this score, but no more adequate definition has yet gained general acceptance.

I also found that numerous non-European peoples, many of whom do rather bright things, had been given intelligence tests by both psychologists and anthropologists with due attention to linguistic and other handicaps and had consistently come out with low IQs. This could mean either that we are of a master race, or else that we are in effect accepting an assumption that there is only one really good way to use the human brain, and that is our way – whatever that may be. Since the latter explanation seemed more reasonable, I endeavored to find out what anthropologists had done to rectify the situation.

More particularly, I hoped to find in the work of anthropologists some substantive research which focused on cultural differences in modes of thinking and problem solving, research which could point to other criteria of intelligence than those valued by European-American professionals. Such studies would permit us to define – and ultimately to measure – different *kinds* of intellectual achievement, rather than, as now, to seek ever more ingenious (or ingenuous) ways of measuring *our* kind of achievement. From this in turn might come a more comprehensive and operationally useful definition of intelligence. However, my conclusion from this search was essentially the one set forth above; emphasis by anthropologists has been almost exclusively on the emotional determinants rather than on the cognitive aspects of personality.

I then turned to re-examine an earlier collaboration with Sarason, a personality and culture study of Truk (Gladwin and Sarason, 1953). We had tried a simplified intelligence test and had at least been enlightened enough to see that it was inappropriate to Trukese perceptual patterns rather than to conclude that their poor performance reflected poor brains. We, or particularly Sarason, had discussed at some length the very concrete, nonabstract nature of Trukese thinking. We earned an honorable mention for that bit of insight, but no medal. A medal was unwarranted for several reasons. First, in my fieldwork I had paid little attention to learning, and no attention to how the Trukese learn to think and learn (Bateson's *deutero-learning*), so we could offer only rather weak speculations as to how this style of thinking developed. Second, we had not developed our analysis of Trukese thinking in a frame of reference such as to command the theoretical attention of other psychologists or anthropologists. We did not, in other words, relate it to theories of cognition and intelligence in a meaningful way. Finally, in undertaking the analytic interpretation of Trukese personality development, I sat just as firmly at the feet of Freud as did any of my contemporaries, in spite of the realization that Trukese thinking and learning was significantly different from that employed by the patients or subjects of Freud or of contemporary psychologists. I did not yet appreciate that if behavior is learned, as we culturally oriented anthropologists keep insisting, the nature of the learning process must have something to do with the kinds of behavior learned.

I cannot in this paper attempt to expiate all my past errors and omissions. Of course I still have no data on how Trukese learn to think. Speculation on the relationship between the nature of learning and the kinds of behavior learned is tempting, but could only be speculation. Instead I shall attempt to place in meaningful perspective the nature of Trukese intellectual achievement, differing as it does from our own in the kinds of thinking employed. Description of a variety of cognitive styles is a necessary first step toward the goal of studying how people learn to think.[2]

In our culture we value (and measure crudely with intelligence tests) relational or abstract thinking, in which bodies of knowledge are integrated and related to each other through unifying symbolic constructs. The Trukese seemingly do not, relying instead on the cumulative product of the adding together of a great number of discrete bits of data, summed together in accordance with predetermined parameters, to arrive at a desired conclusion. Both we and the Trukese operate within a gestalt, a conception of the prob-

2. In preparing the material which follows I have benefited substantially from discussions with Dr Ulric Neisser of Brandeis University. However, I can state with assurance that responsibility for the final product rests with me alone since our discussions had the pleasant attribute of consistently leaving some issue unresolved.

lem as a whole. However, we seek a unifying concept which will comprehend all the relevant facts more or less simultaneously, developing an overall principle or plan from which individual steps toward a solution can be derived deductively. In contrast the Trukese work toward a solution by improvising each step, but always with the final goal in mind. The Trukese start with a simplified gestalt, whether or not they can describe it in words, and fill in the details as they go along. We prefer to look a situation over and design a somewhat special gestalt which will at the outset embrace all the essential details.

If we take as an example the work of the navigator of a sailing canoe, I believe this process will not only become clear, but will also be seen to require a substantial feat of intellect. I say this in spite of the fact that I believe that the Trukese would do badly even on a perceptually appropriate intelligence test, and that in my experience they proved themselves generally incapable of mastering even the relatively simple organizing concept of system functions needed to locate a malfunction in an internal-combustion engine – which they could almost tear down and reassemble blindfolded provided it required only cleaning and overhaul.

Voyages spanning over one hundred miles of open ocean are still made in sailing canoes, and longer ones were made in the past. The destination is often a tiny dot of land less than a mile across, and visible from any distance only because of the height of those coconut trees which may grow in its sandy soil. From a canoe, virtually at the level of the ocean's surface, even a forested island is visible only three or four miles away. To assure that the travellers will come close enough to their destination to sight it after covering miles of empty ocean, with shifting winds and currents, the crew usually rely on one of their number who has been trained in a variety of traditional techniques by an older master navigator, usually a relative of his. These techniques do not include even a compass (although some carry them now for emergencies), to say nothing of chronometer, sextant or star tables.

Essentially the navigator relies on dead reckoning. He sets his course by the rising and setting of stars, having memorized for this purpose the knowledge gleaned from generations of observation of the directions in which stars rise and fall through the seasons. A heading toward a given island, when leaving another island, is set at a particular season a trifle to the left, or perhaps the right, of a certain star at its setting or rising. Through the night a succession of such stars will rise or fall, and each will be noted and the course checked. Between stars, or when the stars are not visible due to daylight or storm, the course is held constant by noting the direction of the wind and the waves. A good navigator can tell by observing wave patterns when the wind is shifting its direction or speed, and by how much. In a dark and starless night the navigator can even tell these things from the sound of the waves as they lap upon the side of the canoe's hull, and the feel of the boat as it travels through the water. All of these complex perceptions – visual, auditory, kinesthetic – are combined with vast amounts of data stored in memory, and the whole is integrated into a slight increase or decrease in pressure on the steering paddle, or a grunted instruction to slack off the sail a trifle.

If the prevailing wind will not permit sailing directly to an island, but requires tacking first in one direction and then in another, the problem becomes even more complex. Tacking involves radical changes in course. While tacking, the canoe is never sailing directly toward its destination, but instead heads considerably to the left and then to the right of a true heading in order to keep the sail filled with wind. Although under conditions of changeable weather (which are common) the navigator may proceed by a series of short tacks which multiply the opportunities for error, the scope of his task can be most readily visualized in terms of a long voyage under a fairly steady but opposing wind. Under these circumstances he may sail for up to a hundred miles on one course, and then make a single turn to a new heading which he will hold, perhaps for a comparable distance, until he sights his destination. The first course, the second course and the point of change are all invisible pathways across the water which have reality only in the mind of the navigator, and for which there are no physical points of reference. Yet when, for example, the change in course is made the navigator must know exactly where he is in the ocean, and where his destination lies, at the time he changes course. This knowledge can only be gained through a cumulative estimate of the rate, time and direction of travel. The course-change may have to occur after two or three days of sailing, out of sight of land and with several shifts in wind velocity and direction. Nevertheless the navigator must change to a new tack within only two or three miles of the ideal point if he is to arrive within sight of the island of his destination.[3] In the old days of European navigation this was done with frequent observations of the compass and of a spinning log line and chronometer, with plottings on a chart. Increasingly now it is accomplished by accelerometers and computers combined into an inertial guidance system. The Trukese navigator, however, does it all in his head. This is an astounding intellectual achievement.

Furthermore, the navigator is likely to have received his training because he happened to have a relative who knew the skills and wanted to keep them in the family, rather than being selected entirely because of his intelligence.

What kind of information is the navigator utilizing, how is he selecting it, and how does he have to manipulate and integrate it in order to produce a useful end product – e.g., differential pressure on the steering paddle? His information consists of a large number of discrete observations, a combination of motion, sounds, feel of the wind, wave patterns, star relationships, etc. Each is a concrete, largely unequivocal factual observation. Either the boat is heading toward the correct star or it is not. The wind is from a certain direction and of a certain velocity; although it takes practice to observe this accurately, the fact is unambiguous. The significance of each observation is established by a comparison with remembered observations from past experience, a result of training. This training and experience also determines unequivocally what phenomena shall be observed and what ignored. The selection and accumulation of necessary information thus requires a minimum of reasoning or logical choice.

It is as routine and automatic as are the observations of a motorist who, for example, is approaching an intersection or curve and

3. Sharp (1957) contends on *a priori* grounds that tacking upwind in this fashion on long voyages is impossible in a sailing canoe without European navigation aids. First-hand testimony by Americans, notably Rev. John K. Fahey, SJ, and Rev. William E. Rively, SJ, refutes this and some of Sharp's other pessimistic conclusions. A number of other authorities also disagree with Sharp (see Golson, 1963).

must decide whether to slow down, stop, shift gears, or whatever. The motorist, almost without conscious thought and often while he is carrying on a conversation, observes and relates to previous experience the visibility, the road surface, the bank of a curve and even the minor cues which suggest that a crossroad is or is not heavily travelled. Furthermore, the highway upon which the motorist is driving may have other traffic. Cars and trucks are travelling in front of and behind him, at different speeds and with different rates of possible acceleration, manoeuverability, etc. Yet if he is an experienced driver he can predict almost exactly where each will be at any given moment. An occasional glance ahead or into the mirror will suffice to keep these position estimates up to date. In other words the motorist simultaneously integrates a large number of estimates of rate, time, direction and distance, plus predictive extensions of these variables, into a constantly changing gestalt which defines his relative position both in the flow of traffic and with respect to the approaching curve in the highway.

This is the same process that is employed by the Trukese navigator. His progress across the ocean is guided by a constant awareness in his own mind of his location relative to the position of every island and reef in the area through which he is travelling. Each bit of information – whether a perception of changed conditions or an awareness of continuing progress under constant conditions – is integrated into a cumulative but changing knowledge of position and travel thus far. The navigator's mental image is analogous to a radar screen on which a moving spot of light shows his position relative to other objects at any moment. His navigational decisions are then made on an *ad hoc* basis to assure continued progress toward his goal. The operational judgments regarding changes in sailing directions would actually be arrived at in exactly the same way if he were constantly within sight of land; the difference lies not in how the boat is handled but in being able to *know* where the landmarks lie without being able to see them.

Contrast this with the more familiar navigational procedures in the European tradition. Western navigators plan their entire voyage in advance. A course is plotted on a chart and this in turn provides the criteria for decision. Progress is assessed at any given moment relative to a position along the plotted line. Unless the navigator is sailing a direct point-to-point course, he does not carry in his mind a physical sense of where he is going. In his mind is an overall plan, and an estimate of the amount of this plan which has thus far been accomplished. He can always draw a line on the chart between his on-course position and his destination, thus determining where he is relative to his goal, but unless someone inquires he need never be aware, as he stands by the helm, just where over the horizon his destination lies.

We have, then, a contrast between two cognitive strategies. One, the European, begins with a single unifying plan which is then implemented piecemeal with minimal further reference to the overall goal synthesized within it (cf. Miller, Galanter and Pribram, 1960). Almost all the thinking is done in advance of its implementation. The other strategy, the Trukese, operates with reference to its beginning and particularly its ending points, and a point between. The point between, the present position of the boat, is constantly being related to the ending point. Each move is successively determined on an *ad hoc* basis. Thinking is continuous, and in our culture we should consider it a series of improvisations. The tools – mechanical aids versus sensory perceptions – are different in the two examples, but either set of tools could within limits serve either strategy.

The contrast is especially clear operationally when external conditions change, forcing a change in sailing directions. The Trukese navigator simply adds the new dimension to his overall perception of the situation and keeps on sailing appropriately toward his destination. The European navigator, however, is forced to depart from his original plan. Before he can change course he must develop a new plan. He expresses this in a new set of course lines between his present position and his destination. Only after he has linked these points together in a new synthesis can he make the first tactical response to the changed conditions.

The European and Trukese cognitive strategies just outlined differ in at least two essential respects. One is that the European procedure can be described fully in words by the navigator. At any time he is prepared to give a 'logical' explanation of what he is doing. He has a complete and adequate plan from which he can deduce each necessary step, even including a new plan. This ability to conceptualize and verbalize a plan is, often implicitly, assumed to be an essential attribute of 'intelligent' behavior as we understand it in our culture. In contrast the Trukese navigator can point to his destination over the horizon, something the European generally cannot do, but he cannot possibly put into words all of the myriad perceptions which have led him to be sure at that moment where the island lies. This is not merely because the Trukese are unaccustomed to describing in words what they are doing. The simultaneous integration of several discrete thought-processes defies verbalization. The navigator can probably inventory all of the factors to which he must be alert, but the process whereby these are weighted and combined is both complex and fluid.

The other difference lies in the logical processes employed by each. The cognitive strategy of the European navigator can be characterized as essentially deductive, proceeding from principles to details. Before he embarks upon a voyage, or upon a new course, he takes into account a number of factors, both general and specific, which will govern his subsequent actions. These may include the condition of his vessel, policies of his organization, the urgency of his cargo, probable weather conditions and an appropriate time of day for arrival at his destination. Out of the possibly conflicting mandates flowing from these considerations he will develop a plan which will incorporate compromises but will constitute his organizing principle of operation. In implementing this plan he will again be governed by navigational and other techniques which are concrete applications of basic principles. Some of these, such as the movement of celestial bodies, are highly abstract in nature and are translatable into a navigational fix only through several steps of deductive logic. The navigator may or may not understand all of the theory which lies behind his techniques, but they had originally to be developed through an explicit sequence of logical steps. However, once the European navigator has developed his operating plan and has available the appropriate technical resources, the implementation and monitoring of his navigation can be accomplished with a minimum of thought. He has simply to perform almost mechanically the steps dictated by his training and by his initial planning synthesis.

It would be satisfying to suggest, in contrast to the European deductive strategy, that the Trukese navigator operates inductively, proceeding from details to principles. He does indeed start with details, but he never arrives at any discernible principles. The details are of several kinds. There are categories of phenomena which he has learned, through training, he must observe. In attending to these he applies criteria, based upon both training and experience, which permit him to evaluate their relative importance. Finally, there are the characteristics of his canoe in its present condition and loading which determine the nature and magnitude of the actions necessary to maintain a desired heading or speed. The input of information (observations) and its synthesis (application of weighting criteria) is a continuous process characteristically involving multiple simultaneous operations. The output takes two forms: decisions relative to handling the canoe, and a constantly changing mental perception of where the canoe lies relative to its destination.

This total process goes forward without reference to any explicit principles and without any planning, unless the intention to proceed to a particular island can be considered a plan. It is nonverbal and does not follow a coherent sequence of logical steps. As such it does not represent what we tend to value in our culture as 'intelligent' behavior. It certainly does not represent the kind of intelligence measured by virtually all intelligence tests. We might refer to this kind of ability as a 'knack', and respect a person for his competence, but we would not on these grounds qualify him as a profound thinker. Yet it is undeniable that the process of navigating from one tiny island to another, when this is accomplished entirely through the mental activity of the navigator, must reflect a high order of intellectual functioning.[4]

I do not wish to raise here the question of whether the Trukese are

4. This lack of preplanning leads to some interesting speculation. The Trukese, in common with probably the majority of non-European peoples, lack a meaningful orientation of the self toward the future. They are not poised to think about the later phases of their life trajectories and are unlikely to consider the long-term consequences of their present behavior. They do not, in other words, plan ahead in their lives. It is tempting to conclude that the lack of future orientation and planning is somehow functionally related to the lack of planning in cognitive or problem-solving activities. However, this must remain entirely speculative until data from other cultures are available.

more or less intelligent in an absolute sense than Europeans. This question will probably always be unanswerable. It certainly will never be answered until we have eliminated the deficit in our knowledge which it is the primary purpose of this paper to underscore. This is an essential lack of clarity, indeed a lack of definition, with respect to the nature of intelligence and of intellectual and cognitive processes. Some psychologists – Bartlett, Bruner, Guilford, Hebb, and Piaget to name a few – are concerned about this lack of clarity and are attempting to develop a basis for a theory of thinking. However, their work immediately strikes an anthropologist as culture-bound. Their starting point is our familiar symbolic logic and relational abstract thinking. They do not have before them a range of other possible basic approaches to thinking, learning and problem solving. In other fields of inquiry into human behavior anthropology has made rich contributions to theoretical perspective and to the documentation of alternative modes of behaviour. But anthropology has permitted the study of intelligence and learning, especially as it is related to education, to develop into a major concern of many nations of the world without giving it more than the most passing attention. Anthropologists stoutly defend the equality of all men, especially with respect to intellectual potential, without any attempt to analyse or document the nature of similarities and differences in thinking. In this vital area we make no cross-cultural comparisons, and indeed have no theoretical framework within which to make them.

My analysis of the work of the Trukese navigator is frankly speculative, and at best is a crude first approximation to what actually goes on in his head. But analyses of this sort, particularly those developed on the basis of fieldwork directed to this end, can have real value in providing just that perspective on cognition which is so sorely needed and which in other contexts is the stock in trade of anthropology.

References

BATESON, G. (1942), 'Social planning and the concept of "Deutero-learning"', in *Conference on Science, Philosophy, and Religion, Second Symposium*, Harper & Row.

BATESON, G. (1958), *Naven*, 2nd edn, Stanford University Press.

GLADWIN, T., and SARASON, S. B. (1953), *Truk: Man in Paradise*, Viking Fund Publications in Anthropology, no. 20, Wenner-Gren Foundation for Anthropological Research, Inc.

GLADWIN, T., and STURTEVANT, W. C. (eds.) (1962), *Anthropology and Human Behavior*, Anthropological Society of Washington.

GOLSON, J. (ed.) (1963), *Polynesian Navigation: A Symposium on Andrew Sharp's Theory of Accidental Voyages*, The Polynesian Society, memoir 34, Wellington.

MASLAND, R. L., SARASON, S. B., and GLADWIN, T. (1958), *Mental Subnormality: Biological, Psychological, and Cultural Factors*, Basic Books.

MILLER, G. A., GALANTER, E., and PRIBRAM, K. H. (1960), *Plans and the Structure of Behavior*, Holt, Rinehart & Winston.

SHARP, A. (1957), *Ancient Voyagers in the Pacific*, Penguin.

TANNER, J. M., and INHELDER, B. (eds.) (1960), *The Proceedings of the Fourth Meeting of the World Health Organization Study Group on the Psychobiological Development of the Child*, vol. 4, International Universities Press, New York.

7 Charles O. Frake
The Diagnosis of Disease among the Subanun of Mindanao

Charles O. Frake, 'The diagnosis of disease among the Subanun of Mindanao', *American Anthropologist,* vol. 63, 1961.

Although my original fieldwork among the Eastern Subanun, a pagan people of the southern Philippines, was focused on a study of social structure, I found it exceedingly difficult to participate in ordinary conversations, or even elicit information within the setting of such conversations, without having mastered the use of terminologies in several fields, notably folk botany and folk medicine, in which I initially had only marginal interest. Effective use of Subanun botanical and medical terminologies required more knowledge of verbal behavior than linguists typically include in their conception of a structural description. To generate utterances which were grammatical (Chomsky, 1957, pp. 13–17) but not necessarily meaningful or congruent (Joos, 1958) did not suffice. Yet descriptive linguistics provides no methods for deriving rules that generate statements which are semantically as well as grammatically acceptable. Having acquired only an unsystematic and intuitive 'feel' for the use of certain portions of the Subanun lexicon during a first field study, I attempted during a second study a more rigorous search for meanings. This investigation became a major focus of my fieldwork. Presented here is a partial analysis of one of the less numerous terminologies: 186 'disease names'. (Single quotation marks enclose *glosses,* English labels which substitute for, *but do not define,* Subanun terms.)[1]

1. Field work among the Subanun, conducted in 1953–4 and 1957–8, was supported by grants from the US Government, Yale South-east Asia Studies Program, and Smith, Kline & French Co. The bulk of the data upon which this analysis is based were obtained in 1957–8 in the Gulu Disakan and Lipay regions north-east of Sindangan Bay in the interior of Zamboanga del Norte Province. All linguistic forms cited are from the

The Subanun

Some 50,000 Eastern Subanun inhabit the eastern portion of Zamboanga Peninsula, a 130 mile-long extension of the island of Mindanao in the Philippines. Most of this population practices swidden farming in the mountainous interior of the peninsula, leaving the coasts to Christian immigrants of recent decades from the Bisayan Islands to the north. Prior to this century the coasts were controlled, and sporadically occupied, by Philippine Moslems, who established an exploitative hegemony over the pagan Subanun in certain locales (Christie, 1909; Frake, 1957b).

In terms of segmentation and stratification, Subanun society displays remarkable simplicity. Each nuclear family is the focus of a partially unique and variable network of social ties with kin and neighbors which constitutes, for that family, the 'total society'. This maximal, nondiscrete sphere of social relationships has no corporate organization and is not segmented into lineages, age-sets, secret societies, territorial districts, political factions, or the like. Despite this simplicity of their social structure, the Subanun carry on constant and elaborate interfamily social activities: litigation, offerings, feasts – all well lubricated with ample quantities of rice wine. Warfare is lacking (Frake, 1961).

All Subanun are full-time farmers. Special statuses are few in number, filled by achievement rather than ascription, restricted in domain and limited in economic rewards. The status of legal authority has been discussed elsewhere (Frake, 1957a). In the sphere of making decisions about disease, differences in individual skill and knowledge receive recognition, but there is no formal status of diagnostician or even, by Subanun conception, of curer. Everyone is his own 'herbalist' (*memulun*). There are religious specialists, 'mediums'

Eastern Subanun dialect of this region. The frequent use of the first person plural in this article is not a rhetorical device but reflects the indispensable participation of my wife, Carolyn M. Frake, in the collection of field data. My handling of this material has profited from lengthy discussons with Harold Conklin and Volney Stefflre. Dell Hymes and Clyde Kluckhohn made helpful criticisms of an earlier draft of this paper.

(*belian*), whose job it is to maintain communications with the very important supernatural constituents of the Subanun universe. Mediums hold curing ceremonies, but the gods effect the cure. They make possible verbal communication with the supernaturals, but again the information received comes from the gods. The medium is but a channel for the divine message.

A consideration of disease etiology, together with etiologically-derived therapy, would require extended discussion of Subanun relations with the supernatural world. In limiting ourselves to diagnosis, on the other hand, we can largely ignore information derived from very noisy, supernaturally-produced signals.

Disease concepts

'Am I sick?' 'What kind of disease do I have?' 'What are my chances?' 'What caused this disease?' 'Why did it happen to me (of all people)?' Illness evokes questions such as these among patients the world over. Every culture provides a set of significant questions, potential answers and procedures for arriving at answers. The cultural answers to these questions are *concepts* of disease. The information necessary to arrive at a specific answer and eliminate others is the *meaning* of a disease concept.

The Subanun patient, no matter how minor his illness, rarely depends upon introspection to answer these questions. He solicits the readily proffered judgement and advice of kin, neighbors, friends, specialists, deities and ethnographers. Sickness comprises the third most frequent topic of casual conversation (after litigation and folk botany) among Subanun of my acquaintance, and it furnishes the overwhelmingly predominant subject of formal interviews with the supernaturals.

Because disease is not only suffered and treated, but also talked about, disease concepts are verbally labelled and readily communicable. Their continual exposure to discussions of sickness facilitates the learning of disease concepts by all Subanun. Subanun medical lore and medical jargon are not esoteric subjects; even a child can distinguish *buni* from *buyayag* – two fungous skin infections not, to my knowledge, differentiated by Western medical science – and state the reasons for his decision.

This corpus of continually-emitted and readily-elicitable verbal behavior about disease provides our evidence for the existence and meaning of culturally defined disease concepts. We begin with actual disease cases – instances of 'being sick' (*miglaru*) by Subanun identification. We note the kinds of questions *the Subanun ask* about these cases, we record the alternative (or *contrasting*) replies to each kind of question, and then we seek to differentiate the factors by which a Subanun decides one reply, rather than an alternative, applies in a particular situation.

Among the questions evoked by a disease case, there invariably appears one of a set of utterances which demands a 'disease name' (*ŋalan mesait en*) in response. Answering a question with a 'disease name' is *diagnosis*. Subanun diagnosis is the procedure of judging similarities and differences among instances of 'being sick', placing new instances into culturally-defined and linguistically-labelled categories. Diagnostic decisions pertain to the selection of 'medicinal' (*kebuluŋan*) therapy, to prognosis and to the assumption of an appropriate sick role by the patient. They do not answer, nor depend upon, the crucial etiological questions that guide the search for 'ritual' (*kanu*) therapy in severe and refractory cases. The Subanun thus discriminate among the various constellations of disease symptoms and react differentially to them. They diagnose *kinds* of disease.

Disease names

The fundamental unit of Subanun diagnosis is the *diagnostic category* (or 'disease') labelled by a 'disease name'. Whereas an *illness* is a single instance of 'being sick', a diagnostic category is a conceptual entity which classifies particular illnesses, symptomatic or pathogenic components of illness, or stages of illness. The course of an illness through time and its symptomatic components at any one time do not always fit into a single diagnostic category. Consequently, a single illness may successively or simultaneously require designation by several disease names.

Although not all illnesses can be diagnosed by a single disease name, every disease name can diagnose a single illness. Disease names thus differ from designations of kinds of symptoms, such as 'itch' (*matel*), or kinds of pathogenic agents, such as 'plant floss' (*glaɲis*), which do not function as diagnostic labels for illnesses.

The question 'What kind of illness is that?' (*dita? gleruun ai run ma iin*) will always elicit a diagnostic description. Actually, however, a Subanun rarely states this question explicitly; rather he implies it when making an assertion such as 'I feel sick' (what do you think is wrong with me?); 'You look sick' (what is the matter with you?); 'I hear he's sick' (do you know what he's got?). When accompanied by the proper intonation and inserted particles to express worried concern, such utterances invariably stimulate diagnostic discussions resulting in a consensual linguistic description of a particular illness.

If none of the linguistic components of a description of an illness can by itself describe a disease case, then the description as a whole constitutes a disease name, labelling a single diagnostic category. Thus the description *mesait gulu* ('headache') labels a single diagnostic category, for neither *mesait* ('pain') nor *gulu* ('head') can alone diagnose an illness. On the other hand, the description *mesait gulu bu? mesait tian* ('headache and stomach ache') constitutes two diagnostic categories because each component can itself serve as a description of an illness. A single disease name is a *minimal* utterance that can answer the query 'What kind of illness is that?'

At the most specific level of contrast (see below), we have recorded 186 human-disease names (apart from referential synonyms), and the productivity of Subanun disease terminology permits the formation of an indefinite number of additional names. For example, we never recorded *mesait kuleŋkay* ('little-finger pain') as a disease name, but should a Subanun find occasion to communicate such a concept he could unambiguously do so by constructing this label.

Standard descriptive phrases of the productive (polylexemic) type, such as *mesait tian* ('stomach ache') and *meŋebag gatay* ('swollen liver'), label a number of common ailments. A few other disease names, which one might call 'suggestive' rather than 'descriptive', have constituents not productive in the formation of new disease names: for example, the derivative *penabud* ('splotchy itch') < *sabud* ('to scatter, as chicken feed'). There remain 132 diagnostic categories which possess unique, single-word labels. The Subanun must consequently rote-learn unique and distinctive labels for the vast majority of his diseases, a situation paralleled even more markedly in the botanical lexicon of well over one thousand items. The fact that all Subanun do, in fact, learn to use such a copious vocabulary of disease and plant terms with great facility reflects the prominent place of these terminologies in daily conversation.

Levels of contrast

In a given diagnostic situation, a Subanun must select one disease name out of a set of contrasting alternatives as appropriately categorizing a given set of symptoms. Before considering his criteria of selection, we must determine which disease categories, in fact, contrast with each other. Two disease names *contrast* if only one can correctly diagnose a particular set of symptoms. (We consider later the question of disagreement about 'correctness'.) A particular illness may require the diagnoses of more than one set of symptoms for complete description, as with the case of 'being sick' with both a 'headache' and a 'stomach ache'. In such cases the linguistic construction with 'and' (*bu?*) makes it clear that the illness comprises a conjunction of two contrasting diagnostic categories. With reference to the set of symptoms of pains in the head, only one of the contrasting responses is applicable. Any difficulties caused by conjunctive descriptions of illnesses can be obviated by taking evidence for contrast only from illnesses described by a single disease name.

When the same set of symptoms elicits different single-disease-name responses, and informants consider each response to be correct, two things may be responsible. The disease names may be referential synonyms; i.e., the categories they designate are mutually inclusive or equivalent. This happens when, for example, the terms are dialect variants or variants appropriate to different kinds of discourse, such as casual as opposed to formal speech. The second possibility, and the one that concerns us here, is that one category totally includes another; it is superordinate and operates at a less specific *level of contrast*.

An example from English illustrates the meaning of *levels of contrast*. If we confront English-speaking informants with a dog, say a poodle, and collect designations applicable to it, we would eventually have a corpus of words such as poodle, dog, animal, and (from the zoologically sophisticated) canine, mammal, vertebrate. Since all of these words correctly designate the same object, they do not contrast at the same level. Neither are they referential synonyms, for whereas all poodles are dogs, the converse is not true. The category 'dog' totally includes the category 'poodle'. A poodle is a kind of dog, a dog a kind of mammal, a mammal a kind of vertebrate, and so on. Arranging classes by inclusion produces a hierarchy of levels, each ascending level being less specific and including more than its predecessor.

Now suppose, still pointing to a poodle, we ask our (zoologically unsophisticated) informants the following questions:

1. 'Is it a plant?'
2. 'Is it a cat?'
3. 'Is it a collie?'

The responses are, respectively:

1. 'No, it's an animal.'
2. 'No, it's a dog.'
3. 'No, it's a poodle.'

Animal thus contrasts with plant, dog with cat, and poodle with collie.

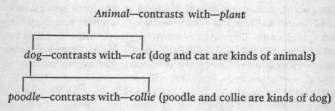

Animal—contrasts with—*plant*

dog—contrasts with—*cat* (dog and cat are kinds of animals)

poodle—contrasts with—*collie* (poodle and collie are kinds of dog)

We could, of course, elicit many more contrasts at each level, and, working with zoologists or dog-lovers as informants, we could isolate additional levels.

A *taxonomic hierarchy* comprises different sets of contrasting categories at successive levels, the categories at any one level being included in a category at the next higher level. Taxonomies divide phenomena into two dimensions: a horizontal one of discrimination (poodle, collie, terrier) and a vertical one of generalization (poodle, dog, animal).

The importance of recognizing levels of contrast in Subanun disease nomenclature first became apparent when, early in the field-work, I had an infectious swelling on my leg. I asked all visitors for the name of my ailment and received a variety of different answers (all single disease names) from different people or even from the same people on different occasions. Subanun disease naming seemed to be an inconsistent and unpredictable jumble. Further interrogation, together with closer attention to the socio-linguistic contexts of responses, soon made it clear that all respondents were right; they were just talking at different levels of contrast. Some – especially those who wished to avoid a detailed medical discussion of my ills in favor of another subject – were simply telling me I had a 'skin disease' (*nuka*) and not another kind of external disease. Others were informing me that I had an 'inflammation' (*meŋebag*) and not some other 'skin disease'. Still others – habitual taxonomic hair-splitters and those who had therapeutic recommendations in mind – were diagnosing the case as 'inflamed quasi bite' (*pagid*) and not some other kind of 'inflammation'.

Figure 1 diagrams the taxonomic structure of a portion of the twenty-nine specific 'skin disease' (*nuka*) categories. Superordinate categories stand above their subordinates. A given category contrasts with another category at the level at which the two share an upper horizontal boundary not crossed by a vertical boundary. Any case, for example, diagnosed as *telemaw glai* ('shallow distal ulcer') can also be labelled *telemaw* ('distal ulcer'), *beldut* ('sore'), or *nuka* ('skin disease') depending on the contrastive context. If, pointing to a ('shallow distal ulcer'), one asks:

1. Is it a *telemaw glibun* ('deep distal ulcer')?
2. Is it a *baga ?* ('proximal ulcer')?
3. Is it a *meŋebag* ('inflammation')?
4. Is it a *samad* ('wound')?

the predictable responses are respectively:

1. No, it's a *telemaw glai* ('shallow distal ulcer')
2. No, it's a *telemaw* ('distal ulcer')

samad 'wound'	nuka 'skin disease'													
						beldut 'sore'								
			meŋebag 'inflammation'			telemaw 'distal ulcer'		baga? 'proximal ulcer'					buni 'ring-worm'	
	pugu 'rash'	nuka 'eruption'	pagid 'inflamed quasi bite'	bekukaŋ 'ulcerated inflammation'	meŋebag 'inflamed wound'	telemaw glai 'shallow distal ulcer'	telemaw bligun 'deep distal ulcer'	baga? 'shallow proximal ulcer'	begwak 'deep proximal ulcer'	beldut 'simple sore'	selimbunut 'spreading sore'	buyayag 'exposed ringworm'	buni 'hidden ringworm'	bugais 'spreading itch'

Figure I Levels of contrast in 'skin disease' terminology

3. No, it's a *beldut* ('sore').
4. No, it's a *nuka* ('skin disease').

The clearest examples of different levels of contrast appear when a disease category subdivides into 'varieties'. Systemic conditions producing discolored urine, for example, known generally as *glegbay*, have 'red' (*glegbay gempula*) and 'white' (*glegbay gemputi?*) subcategories. The 'distal ulcer' (*telemaw*) subdivides into *telemaw glai* ('male [i.e., shallow] ulcer') and *telemaw glibun* ('female [i.e., deep] ulcer'). Although in these examples, subordinate levels of contrast are indicated by attaching attributes to superordinate disease names, such linguistic constructions are not necessarily evidence of inclusion. Thus *beldut pesui* ('sty', literally, 'chick sore'), is not a kind of *beldut* ('sore') but a kind of 'eye disease' (*mesait mata*). It is the way linguistic labels are applied to phenomena and not the linguistic structure of those labels that points to levels of contrast.

As a matter of fact, when we systematically investigate the contrasts of each Subanun disease term, we find a number of cases in which the same linguistic form appears at different levels of contrast. The term *nuka* ('skin disease') for example not only denotes a general category of ailments which includes conditions like *baga?* ('ulcer') but it also denotes a specific kind of skin condition, a mild 'eruption' that contrasts with *baga?* (see Figure 1). In all such cases, if the context (especially the eliciting utterance) does not make the level of contrast clear, respondents can indicate the more specific of two levels by means of optional particles: e.g., *tantu nuka* 'real *nuka*', i.e., 'eruption', not *any* 'skin disease'.

The use of the same linguistic form at different levels of contrast, while a source of confusion until one attends to the total context in which a term is used, should not surprise us. It is common enough in English. The word *man*, for example, designates at one level a category contrasting with nonhuman organisms. At a more specific level, *man* designates a subcategory of human organisms contrasting with *woman*. Subordinate to this we find the contrast: *man* (adult male) – *boy*. *Man* can even appear at a still more specific level to designate a kind of adult male human, as in Kipling's '. . . you'll be a man, my son'.

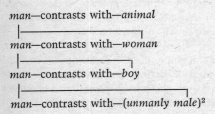

This use of single forms at several levels of contrast seems particularly characteristic of Subanun disease terminology. It appears elsewhere as well, in botanical nomenclature and kinship terminology for instance, but not so extensively. The reasons for its use in disease terminology become, in part, explicable when we consider the use of disease names to designate sequential stages of illness.

The changing and unpredictable course of disease symptoms considerably complicates diagnosis. Of course, other phenomena also change. A plant, passing from seedling to mature tree, changes rad-

2. There is no standard lexeme labelling the category that contrasts with *man* in the sense of manly male. The most likely polylexemic designation is probably 'not a real man'.

ically in appearance. But a seedling of one kind invariably produces a mature plant of the same kind. A papaya seedling never grows into a mango tree. Consequently, the members of a plant category can be identified at any stage of growth, and terminological distinctions of growth stages do not affect classifications of kinds of plants. Given an illness at a particular stage of development, on the other hand, its symptoms may proceed along a variety of different courses or it may heal altogether. Just as one illness sometimes requires several disease names for complete description at any one time, so its course over time may pass through several distinct diagnostic categories.

Every disease name designates a potential *terminal* stage: a stage of 'being sick' immediately preceding 'cure' (or 'recuperation') or 'death'. But some disease stages, potentially terminal, may also be prodromal stages of other terminal diagnostic categories. This situation occurs especially among the skin diseases. Each sequential stage leading to an ulcer or an itchy skin disease is, in itself, a potential terminal stage designated by a disease name. A case of *nuka* ('eruption'), for example, sometimes heals without complication; at other times it eventually develops into one of twenty-three more serious diseases. Consequently, *nuka* not only designates a terminal disease category but also a stage of development in a variety of other diseases.

Figure 2 shows that *nuka* is the pivotal stage in the development of the majority of 'skin diseases'. And it is this term that also serves as a general designation for 'skin diseases', including some for which *nuka* ('eruption') is not a prodrome.

The term *nuka* thus has three uses:

1. as a general designation for 'skin disease', applicable to any skin disease at any stage of development;
2. to designate a prior stage of some, but not all, 'skin diseases';
3. to label a terminal diagnostic category, 'eruption', which contrasts with other 'skin-disease' categories.

The reader will find further examples of multiple semantic uses of single linguistic forms by comparing Figures 1 and 2.

Subanun disease terminology well illustrates the proviso, often stated but rarely followed through in semantic analysis, that the meaning of a linguistic form is a function of the total situation, linguistic and nonlinguistic, in which the form is used. Essentially it is a matter of determining with what a term contrasts in a particular situation. When someone says, 'This is an *x*', what is he saying it is *not*? (cf. Kelly, 1955, pp. 59–64).

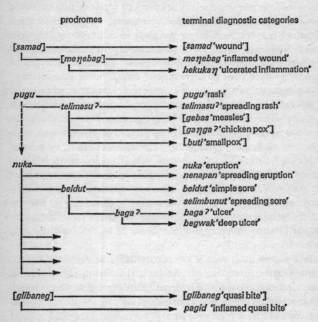

Figure 2 Skin disease stages
Only a few of the diseases arising from *nuka* ('eruption') are shown. Diseases enclosed in brackets are not classifiable as *nuka* ('skin disease').

Figures 1 and 2 reveal a partial relation between levels of contrast and stages of development in 'skin disease' terminology. Among 'skin diseases', where the course of development *through different diagnostic categories* is most complex, the segregation of different levels of contrast is more elaborate than elsewhere in the disease taxonomy. But the terminological complexity of skin disease development does not suffice to explain why this area of the disease vocabulary exhibits more levels of contrast than other areas. A similar variability of number of levels in different segments of a taxonomy, not correlated with the designation of developmental stages, also occurs in botanical and zoological nomenclature.

To explain why some areas of a folk taxonomy subdivide into a greater number of superordinate-subordinate levels than others, we advance the following hypothesis: the greater the number of distinct social contexts in which information about a particular phenomenon must be communicated, the greater the number of different levels of contrast into which that phenomenon is categorized. Skin diseases, for example, enter into a wide variety of social contexts, apart from therapeutically oriented discussions. They can influence bride-price calculations. Here, the concern is over the degree of disfigurement and the contagiousness of the disease. They can be used to justify, perhaps to one's spouse, a failure to perform an expected task. Here the disabling properties of the disease must be communicated. Skin disease terms figure prominently in competitive joking and maligning, thus entering into special kinds of discourse such as drinking songs and verse. In many of these situations it is imperative to speak at just the level of generality that specifies the pertinent information but leaves other, possibly embarrassing, information ambiguous.

The same hypothesis should hold cross-culturally. If the botanical taxonomy of tribe A has more levels of contrast than that of tribe B, it means that the members of tribe A communicate botanical information in a wider variety of socio-cultural settings. It does not mean that people in tribe A have greater powers of 'abstract thinking'. As a matter of fact it says nothing about general differences in cognition, for when it comes to fish, tribe B may reveal the greater number of levels of contrast.

Folk taxonomies are cultural phenomena. Their structural variation within and between cultures must be explained by the cultural uses to which a taxonomy is put, and not by appeal to differences in the cognitive powers of individual minds (cf. Brown, 1958, pp. 284–5).

Diagnostic criteria

A 'disease name', it will be recalled, is a minimal, congruent (i.e., meaningful) answer to the question, 'What kind of illness is that?' (*ditaʔ gleruun ai run ma iin*). Alternatively, it is a congruent insertion in the frame, 'The name of (his) disease is ———' (*zalan en ig mesait en* ———). Since different *illnesses*, that is, different instances of 'being sick' (*miglaru*), may elicit the same disease-name response, a disease name labels a class of illnesses: a *diagnostic category*.

Given a set of contrasting disease names, the problem remains of determining the rules which govern the assigning of one name rather than another in a particular diagnostic situation. Rules of use may be analytic, perceptual or explicit in derivation.

Analytic derivation of meanings ideally yields *distinctive features*: necessary and sufficient conditions by which an investigator can determine whether a newly encountered instance is or is not a member of a particular category. The procedure requires an independent, *etic* (Pike, 1954, p. 8) way of coding recorded instances of a category. Examples are the 'phone types' of linguistics and the 'kin types' of kinship analysis (Lounsbury, 1956, pp. 191–2). The investigator classifies his data into types of his own formulation, then compares 'types' *as though* they were instances of a concept. From information already coded in the definitions of his 'types', he derives the necessary and sufficient conditions of class membership. Thus by comparing the kin types of English 'uncle' (FaBr, MoBr, FaSiHu, etc.) with the kin types in every other English kin category, the analyst finds that by scoring 'uncle' for features along four dimensions of contrast (affinity,[3] collaterality, generation and sex) he can state succinctly how 'uncles' differ from every other category of kinsmen. The definition of 'uncle' as 'non-affinal, first-degree collateral, ascending generation male' suffices to enable an investigator

---

3. English kinship classification requires a special definition of affinity to contrast 'in-laws' with other kin, some of whom (like FaSiHu) are conected to ego by a marriage link but are categorized with consanguineals (like FaBr). This definition provides that kin of different generations connected by a marriage link qualify as affinals only if the marriage link is in the lower generation.

to predict whether any new kin type he encounters (such as FaM-oSiHu) is or is not an uncle. This is not, however, the same thing as a definition which states how people in the society in fact categorize persons as 'uncles' (Wallace and Atkins, 1960, pp. 75–9). (When analytically derived features are probabilistically, rather than necessarily and sufficiently, associated with category membership, then we may speak of *correlates* rather than of distinctive features. A correlate of the uncle–nephew relation is that uncles are usually, but not necessarily, older than their nephews.)

To arrive at rules of use one can also direct attention to the actual stimulus discriminations made by informants when categorizing. What perceptual information enables one to distinguish an oak tree from a maple tree, a cold from the flu? Perceptual attributes relevant to categorization, whether distinctive or probabilistic, are *cues*. Discovering cues in ethnographic settings requires as yet largely unformulated procedures of perceptual testing that do not replace the culturally relevant stimuli with artificial laboratory stimuli (cf. Conklin, 1955, p. 342).

Finally, one can simply ask his informants about meanings: 'What is an uncle?' 'How do you know he is an uncle and not a father?' Such procedures yield the culture's explicit definitions or *criteria* of categories (cf. Bruner's [1956, p. 30] 'defining attributes' and Wittgenstein's [1958, pp. 24–5] use of 'criteria' and 'symptoms', the former being distinctive, the latter probabilistic).

These different procedures for determining rules of use are not equally applicable to every system of contrasting categories. Distinctive-feature analysis becomes impractical without an economical, minimally redundant and highly specific etic coding device. Explicit criteria may be lacking or highly inconsistent where category discriminations and decisions do not require verbal description. In some cases, consistent criteria may be present, yet provide an unsatisfactory description of behavior: compare the inutility of seeking informants' explanations in certain tasks of formal linguistic analysis. Yet there are categories – like those pertaining to supernatural phenomena – which are known only through verbal descriptions by informants. The difference between a 'deity' (*diwata*) and a 'goblin' (*menemad*) can only be what my informants tell me it is.

Our choice of procedures for arriving at meanings of disease names is, in part, a function of the kind of category such names label, and, in part, of the kind of field data we succeeded in obtaining about diagnostic behavior.

Distinctive-feature analysis is ruled out on both counts. The preliminary denotative definitions would require a listing of illnesses assigned to each disease category in recorded diagnoses. The only meaningful etic units available for such a list are the diagnostic categories of Western medicine. Practical and methodological problems prevent their use. We had neither facilities nor personnel to make competent Western diagnoses of all disease cases we observed. Yet, useful as such information would be for many other purposes, it would, in fact, prove of little help in defining Subanun diagnostic categories. For one thing, too few illnesses actually occurred during our stay in the field to sample adequately a sufficient proportion of Subanun diagnostic categories. Moreover, even if one could match each Subanun diagnostic category with a series of Western diagnoses, the latter would still provide very deficient etic types. We cannot assume, as we can when working with phone types or kin types, that every Western diagnostic category will be totally included by some Subanun category. Every case diagnosed by Western criteria as tuberculosis will not receive the same Subanun diagnosis. Furthermore, a Subanun category such as *peglekebuun* ('chronic cough') which sometimes matches with tuberculosis, will not always do so. The criteria and cues of the two diagnostic systems are too disparate for one-to-one or one-to-many matching. The problems presented to the analyst by this overlapping of categories in the two systems are compounded by the superabundance of information encoded in a Western diagnostic category. Knowing only that Subanun disease X partially matched Western diagnostic categories *a, b, c,* and that Subanun disease Y partially matched Western categories *d* and *e*, one could not easily extract from medical knowledge about *a, b, c, d* and *e* distinctive features defining the contrast between X and Y. For all of these reasons, distinctive-feature analysis from lists of matched native and scientific names is not feasible for folk taxonomies of disease nor, for that matter, of plants, animals and most other natural phenomena as well.

Inadequacies of our data largely prevent confident definition of Subanun diagnostic categories by distinctive stimulus attributes, or

cues, of illnesses. The discovery of what cue discriminations informants are making when contrasting one disease with another is exceedingly difficult. Many apparently pertinent cues, such as the ones
that enable a Subanun patient to distinguish 'headache' (*mesait
gulu*) from 'migraine' (*tampiak*) are known only by verbal descriptions. A disease 'entity' such as 'headache' is not something that can
be pointed to, nor can exemplars of disease ordinarily be brought
together for visual comparison and contrast as can, say, two plants.
Moreover, situational features other than stimulus attributes of the
illness bear on the final diagnostic decision. The same degree of pain,
if objectively measured, could probably lead to a diagnosis of either
'headache' or 'migraine' depending on current social or ecological
role-demands on the patient. Nevertheless, very few diagnostic decisions are made by the Subanun without some apparent appeal to
stimulus properties of illness; and in the majority of diagnoses these
are the overriding considerations.

It is difficult, then, to define Subanun diagnostic categories in
terms of analytic or perceptual attributes of their denotata. On the
other hand, these very difficulties facilitate recognition of diagnostic
criteria: explicit defining attributes of disease categories. Since one
cannot point to a disease entity and say 'that's a such and such', as
one can with a plant specimen, and since no one individual ever
personally experiences but a fraction of the total number of diseases
he can, in fact, differentiate, the Subanun themselves must learn to
diagnose diseases through verbal description of their significant attributes. It is thus relatively easy for a Subanun to describe precisely
what makes one disease different from another. He can tell us, for
example, that the ulcer *begwak* produces a marked cavity, unlike the
ulcer *baga?* He can describe the difference in appearance between
glepap ('plaque itch') and *penabud* ('splotchy itch'), the difference in
locale between the 'ringworms' *buni* and *buyayag*, the difference in
pathogenesis between *meyebag* (an 'inflamed wound') and *beldut* (a
spontaneous 'sore'). This is not to say that the evaluation of the cues
of a particular illness as exemplars of diagnostic criteria is always
easy or consistent. Informants operating with identical diagnostic
concepts may disagree about the application of these concepts in a
particular case, but they rarely disagree in their verbal definitions of
the concepts themselves.

The procedures for eliciting and analysing diagnostic criteria parallel those used to determine the system of nomenclature: we collect contrasting answers to the questions the Subanun ask when diagnosing disease. By asking informants to describe differences between diseases, by asking why particular illnesses are diagnosed as such and such and not something else, by following discussions among the Sabanun themselves when diagnosing cases, and by noting corrections made of our own diagnostic efforts, we can isolate a limited number of diagnostic questions and criterial answers.

A classification of Subanun diagnostic criteria follows from (1) the questions which elicit them and (2) the status of the answers as diagnostic labels.

1. By eliciting question
1.1. Pathogenic criteria.
1.2. Prodromal criteria.
1.3. Symptomatic criteria.
1.4. Etiological criteria.
2. By status of the answer as a diagnostic label
2.1. Elementary criteria.
2.2. Complex criteria.

1.1. *Pathogenic criteria* are diagnostically significant responses to questions of 'pathogenesis' (*meksamet*), which is different from 'etiology' (*melabet*). 'Pathogenesis' refers to the agent or mechanism that produces or aggravates an illness, 'etiology' to the circumstances that lead a particular patient to contract an illness. Thirty-four elementary diagnostic categories require pathogenic information for diagnosis. Examples are 'wound' (*samad*), 'burn' (*pasu?*), 'intestinal worm' (*bulilaŋ*), 'skin worm' (*tayeb*), 'pinworm' (*glelugay*), 'exposure sickness' (*pasemu*[4]). In such cases, where the identification of a pathogen is criterial to diagnosis, the association between the pathogen and the illness is relatively obvious both to the investigator and to his informants.

4. Latin Americanists should recognize this term (see Redfield and Redfield, 1940, p. 65). Disease names adopted from Spanish *pasmo* or *pasma* are widespread in the Philippines. This was the only Subanun disease name of obvious Spanish origin that we recorded.

In addition, the Subanun posit the existence of many pathogens – such as 'plant floss' (*glaŋis*), 'microscopic mites' (*kamu*), 'intrusive objects' (*meneled*), 'symbolic acts' (*pelii*), 'stress' (*pegendekan*), 'soul loss' (*panaw i gimuud*) – which are not diagnostically criterial. These noncriterial pathogens, whose presence generally must be determined independently of diagnosis, provide clues in the search for etiological circumstances and serve as guides to prophylactic measures. But standard, named pathogens, whether criterial or not, have a limited range of pertinence. In the cognitive decisions occasioned by an illness, pathogenic mechanisms are significant only when they are necessary appurtenances to diagnosis or to etiological explanations. Otherwise they are of little interest. Like Western physicians, the Subanun do not know the pathogenic agents of many of their diseases, but, unlike the former, the Subanun consider this lack of knowledge to be of trivial rather than of crucial therapeutic significance. Consequently a large number of Subanun diseases lack standard pathogenic explanations, and many disease cases go by without any effort (except by the ethnographer) to elicit them from consultants or supernaturals.

1.2. *Prodromal criteria* are diagnostically significant responses to questions of the origin of 'prodrome' (*puunan en*) of a given illness, the 'prodrome' always referring to a prior and diagnostically distinct condition. A *derivative* disease is one whose diagnosis depends on its having a specified prodrome. When referring to a derivative disease, a query about its prodrome *must be* answered by another disease name, previously applicable to the illness. A *spontaneous* disease, in contrast, is one for which the response to a query about prodromes *can be* 'there is no prodrome' (*ndaˀ ig puunan en*).

Figure 2 shows a number of illnesses whose diagnoses depend on their having passed through specific other stages. One cannot have *begwak* ('deep ulcer') unless one has previously, as part of the same 'illness', had *nuka* ('eruption'), *beldut* ('sore'), and *bagaˀ* ('ulcer'), in that order. 'Eruption' (*nuka*), on the other hand, need have no prodrome, though it sometimes begins as 'rash' (*pugu*). The latter disease is always spontaneous.

For any derivative disease, a given prodrome is a necessary but not a sufficient diagnostic criterion. If the evidence of other criteria overwhelmingly points to a contrary diagnosis, one must conclude – since the criteriality of the prodrome cannot be discounted – that the previous diagnosis, or current information about it, is erroneous. Thus an informant insisted that an inflammation on my leg was an inflamed insect bite (*pagid*) rather than an inflamed wound (*tantu meɲebag*), even though I had told him I thought it originated as a 'minor cut'. I simply, according to him, had not noticed the prodromal bite. In such cases the existence of the prodrome is deduced from its criteriality to a diagnosis actually arrived at on other grounds. Our data would have been much improved had we earlier recognized the importance of these *ex post facto* classificatory decisions as evidence of criteriality.

1.3. *Symptomatic criteria* are diagnostically significant responses to a variety of questions about the attributes of an illness currently perceptible to patient or observer. These are the most frequent, wide-ranging and complex of diagnostic criteria. Our data are not, in fact, complete enough to list, or even to enumerate, all the questions, with all their contrasting responses, necessary to define in explicit Subanun terms the symptomatic differences among all disease categories. Moreover, we can present here, in analysed form, only a small proportion of the data we do have.

To exemplify symptomatic criteria we shall discuss several major questions that occur repeatedly in the diagnosis of a variety of illnesses; then we shall illustrate how these and other criterial contrasts intersect to define a segment of skin-disease terminology.

Specifications of locale along several dimensions provide fundamental criteria of Subanun diagnosis, closely relating to selection of appropriate therapeutic measures, to prognostic judgement and to the evaluation of the disabling potential of an illness. First of all, disease symptoms can be located along a dimension of depth or penetration with two basic contrasts: 'external' (*dibabaw*) and 'internal' (*dialem*), depending on the presence or absence of visible lesions on the surface of the body. An external disease may penetrate to produce internal symptoms as well as external lesions, in which case the disease has 'sunk' (*milegdaɲ*). Rarely, a disease may penetrate to the other side of the body producing 'balancing' (*mitimpaɲ*) or 'pierced' (*milapus*) lesions. Penetration is prognostic of seriousness; the therapy of a number of skin diseases aims at preventing 'sinking'.

Those diseases which may be pinpointed anatomically (in Subanun terms, of course) are *localized* diseases. Should an initially localized condition begin to spread to adjacent areas within the same penetration level, then it will often fall into a new and distinct disease category. The distinction between circumscribed and spreading conditions pertains especially to external lesions. If a 'sore' (*beldut*) becomes multilesional (*misarak*), it is no longer *beldut*, but *selimbunut* 'spreading sore'. Other diseases for which spreading is an important diagnostic criterion are 'spreading rash' (*telimasu?*), 'spreading eruption' (*nenapan*), 'yaws' (*buketaw*) and 'spreading itch' (*bugais*). The Subanun describe an external condition that covers all or most of the body surface as *mipugus* or *miluup*, the latter term also designating a completely dibbled rice field.

Degree of penetration and spreading correlate closely with prognostic severity, hence their diagnostic importance. Distinctions of specific locales seem to reflect in part the disabling potential of a disease. Thus, lesions on the hands and feet often receive different designations from similar lesions elsewhere on the body; compare *baga?* ('proximal ulcer') with *telemaw* ('distal ulcer'). Among itchy skin diseases which seldom cause severe discomfort, distinctions of locale correspond with unsightliness. Thus the Subanun, who regard these diseases as extremely disfiguring, distinguish lesions hidden by clothing from those visible on a clothed body: compare *buni* ('hidden ringworm') with *buyayag* ('exposed ringworm').

Specifications of interior locales usually refer to the area below an external reference point: the 'head', 'chest', 'xiphoid', 'side', 'waist', 'abdomen', and so on. The only internal organs commonly named as disease locales are the 'liver' and the 'spleen'. The liver in Subanun anatomical conceptions is somewhat akin to the heart in popular Western notions. (We recorded no Subanun diseases attributed to the heart.) The choice of the spleen as a disease locale seems to represent an instance of Subanun medical acumen. The term for spleen, *nalip* (identified during dissections of pigs), names a disease characterized by externally visible or palpable swelling attributed to this organ. The Subanun regard *nalip* as a complication of actual or latent malaria (*taig*). In Western medicine, an enlarged spleen (splenomegaly) may indicate malaria infection (Shattuck, 1951, p. 50).

Most peoples probably single out disorders of sensation as one of the most pertinent characteristics of diseases: witness our own stock query, 'How are you feeling?' The Subanun ask 'Does it hurt?' (*mesait ma*). The contrasting replies to this question are, first, an affirmative, 'Yes, it hurts'; second, a denial of pain followed by a specification of a contrasting, nonpainful, but still abnormal sensation, 'No, it doesn't hurt; it itches'; and, third, a blanket negation implying no abnormal sensation. Thus the Subanun labels a number of contrasting types of sensation and uses them to characterize and differentiate diseases.

The contrast between 'pain' (*mesait* or *megeel*) and 'itch' or 'irritation' (*matel*) has special relevance to skin lesions. 'Sores' 'hurt', whereas scaly lesions 'itch'. But should a sore-like lesion both 'itch' and at the same time multiply and spread, a distinctive and serious disease is indicated: *buketaw* ('yaws'). The type of sensation also indicates possible pathogenic agents. Pain usually follows some kind of trauma so if the patient has suffered no obvious injury, the supernaturals have very likely inflicted an invisible wound. Itchiness signals the presence of an irritating agent, often *glaŋis* ('plant floss').

Once a condition has been labelled 'painful' in contrast to other possibilities, the kind of pain can be specified as a subordinate level of contrast. However, the Subanun make such specifications more in contexts of complaining about discomfort than in diagnosing. Consequently the terms descriptive of pain are often chosen for their rhetorical rather than denotative value. Such terms resemble English metaphors: 'burning', 'piercing', 'splitting', 'throbbing'.

There are, of course, many other sensations criterial to diagnosis and a long list of diagnostic questions referring to appearances and to bodily functions. Rather than attempting to discuss each of these, it will be of greater methodological advantage to illustrate how a series of questions with their contrasting answers defines one small segment of the disease terminology. Figure 3 diagrams the criterial definitions of the types of 'sores' (*beldut*) distinguished by the Subanun (cf. Figure 1). The 'sores' contrast with 'inflammations' (*meŋebag*) in having the prodrome *nuka* ('eruption'). 'Inflammations' and 'sores', on the other hand, fall together in contrast to many other skin diseases in being 'painful' (*mesait*) rather than 'itchy' (*matel*). Answers to questions of spread, severity, distality (hands and feet *vs* rest of body) and depth differentiate all the sores.

Depth, and especially severity, are not sharply defined by distinctive cues. In the case of 'sores', size, persistence and a variety of specific symptoms may point to severity: suppuration (*dun ig mata nen*), opening (*miterak*), hot sensation (*minit*), throbbing pain (*kendutendut*), intermittent burning pain (*metik*). Although not explicitly stated, judgment of severity is, in fact, partially a function of social-role contingencies. Do the patient and his consultants wish to emphasize the former's crippling disability, which prevent him from discharging an expected obligation? Or do they wish to communicate that the patient's lesion is not serious enough to interfere with his duties? Diagnosis is not an automatic response to

	beldut 'sore'					
	telemaw 'distal ulcer'		*baga ?* 'proximal ulcer'			
levels of terminological contrast	*telemaw gi'ai* 'shallow distal ulcer'	*telemaw gibun* 'deep distal ulcer'	*baga ?* 'shallow proximal ulcer'	*begwak* 'deep proximal ulcer'	*beldut* 'simple sore'	*selimbunut* 'multiple sore'
depth	sh	dp	sh	dp		
distality	distal		proximal			
severity	severe				mild	multiple
spread	single					
diagnostic questions	range of contrasting answers					

Figure 3 Criterial contrasts differentiating the 'sores'

pathological stimuli; it is a social activity whose results hinge in part on role-playing strategies.

1.4. *Etiological criteria* are diagnostically significant responses to questions of 'etiology'; how did the patient 'encounter' (*melabet*) his illness? These questions ask 'Why did it happen to me?' rather than 'What causes this kind of disease?' Diagnostic knowledge of the kind of disease does not give knowledge of 'etiology' in this sense. Confident determination of etiological circumstances requires communication by divination or seance with the supernaturals. Since this kind of communication tends to be costly, patients reserve etiological searching for cases when ordinary 'medicinal' (*kebuluŋan*) treatments predicated on diagnosis have not met with success. Etiological determination generally enables the patient to undertake propitiatory rituals (*kanu*) with therapeutic value. But some etiological circumstances, notably those involving human agency, cannot be counteracted by propitiations to supernaturals. These cases require treatment with specially acquired 'medicines' such as 'charms' (*pegbeliŋen*), 'amulets' (*bulun penapu*), 'potions' (*gaplas*) and 'antidotes' (*tekuliʔ*). When illnesses have a medicinally treatable etiology, the disease is then *named* for the etiological circumstance regardless of previous symptomatic diagnosis. There are seven such diseases, only two of which were recorded as diagnoses during my two years in the field: *mibuyag* ('bewitched') and *pigbuluŋan* ('poisoned').

In view of other descriptions of primitive medicine, the surprising fact about Subanun diagnosis is that in naming all but seven of the 186 human disease categories, diagnostic questions refer directly to the empirical evidence of the disease itself and its history. The exceptional cases result from these few etiological circumstances whose determination by divination or seance necessitates renaming the illness they caused. Otherwise the results of etiological determinations do not affect previously determined empirical diagnoses. A deity may have to inform a Subanun how and why he got sick, but the symptoms themselves normally provide the information to name the disease, and by naming it, the Subanun is well on the road to prognosis and preliminary therapy.

2.1. *Elementary criteria* are those whose linguistic expression is not a disease name. 'Pain' (*mesait*) is an elementary criterion because *mesait*, by itself, cannot function as a disease name.

2.2. *Complex criteria* are themselves diagnostic categories labelled by a disease name. 'Malaria' (*taig*), for example, is diagnosed by the presence of the *disease* 'fever' (*panas*) plus the elementary criterion of 'periodic chills' (*selezaun*). The disease 'fever' (*panas*) is, in turn, diagnosed by the presence of the disease 'malaise' (*mesait glawas*) plus the elementary criterion of 'feeling feverish' (*mpanas*). Earlier we noted that some illnesses require a simultaneous conjunctive description by more than one disease name, e.g., 'stomach ache and headache'. A few conjunctive combinations diagnose distinct disease categories. The diseases 'stomach ache' (*mesait tian*), 'difficult breathing' (*bektus*) and 'chest pains' (*mesait gegdeb*) function as complex criteria in the diagnosis of *ba?us*, a systemic disease for which we have devised no satisfactory gloss.

The significance of diagnosis

The diagnostic criteria distinguishing one Subanun disease from another, in their explicit verbal formulation by informants, define conceptually distinct, mutually exclusive categories at each level of contrast. Informants rarely disagree in their verbal descriptions of what makes one disease different from another. This does not mean, however, that they are equally consistent in their naming of actual disease cases. Two informants may agree that the ulcers *baga?* and *begwak* differ in degree of penetration, yet disagree on whether a particular ulcer they are examining exhibits sufficient depth to exemplify *begwak*. The 'real' world of disease presents a continuum of symptomatic variation which does not always fit neatly into conceptual pigeonholes. Consequently the diagnosis of a particular condition may evoke considerable debate: one reason a patient normally solicits diagnostic advice from a variety of people. But the debate does not concern the definition of a diagnostic category, for that is clear and well known; it concerns the exemplariness of a particular set of symptoms to the definition (cf: Goodenough 1956, p. 215).

Conceptually the disease world, like the plant world, exhaustively divides into a set of mutually exclusive categories. Ideally every illness either fits into one category or is describable as a conjunction of several categories. Subanun may debate, or not know, the place-ment of a particular case, but to their minds that reflects a deficiency in their individual knowledge, not a deficiency in the classificatory system. As long as he accepts it as part of his habitat and not 'foreign', a Subanun, when confronted with an illness, a plant or an animal, may say he does not know the name. He will even say there is no name. The conceptual exhaustiveness of the Subanun classification of natural phenomena contrasts with the re-ported situation among many other peoples.

Diagnosis – the decision of what 'name' to apply to an instance of 'being sick' – is a pivotal cognitive step in the selection of culturally appropriate responses to illness by the Subanun. It bears directly on the selection of ordinary, botanically-derived, medicinal remedies from 724 recorded alternatives. The results of this selection, in turn, influence efforts to reach prognostic and etiological decisions, which, in their turn, govern the possible therapeutic need for a variant of one of sixty-one basic, named types of propitiatory offerings. All of these decisions and resulting actions can have far-reaching social and economic consequences.

In this paper we have presented some methodological devices which we feel are effective in delimiting the basis for decisions underlying terminology systems. Unfortunately, while in the field we did not reach even the methodological sophistication of this article. Consequently, our data have proved deficient at a number of critical points.

References

BROWN, R. (1958), *Words and Things,* Free Press.

BRUNER, J. S., GOODNOW, J. J., and AUSTIN, G. A. (1956), *A Study of Thinking,* Wiley & Sons.

CHOMSKY, N. (1957), *Syntactic Structures,* Mouton.

CHRISTIE, E. B. (1909), *The Subanun of Sindangan Bay,* Bureau of Science, Division of Ethnology Publications, no. 6, Manila.

CONKLIN, H. C. (1955), 'Hanunóo color categories', *Southwestern Journal of Anthropology,* vol. 11, pp. 339–44.

FRAKE, C. O. (1957a), 'Litigation in Lipay: a study in Subanun law', in *Proceedings of the Ninth Pacific Science Congress,* Bangkok.

FRAKE, C. O. (1956), 'The Subanun of Zamboanga: a linguistic survey', in *Proceedings of the Ninth Pacific Science Congress*, Bangkok.

FRAKE, C. O. (1961), 'Family and kinship among the eastern Subanun', in G. P. Murdock (ed.), *Social Structure in Southeast Asia*, Quadrangle, Chicago.

GOODENOUGH, W. G. (1956), 'Componential analysis and the study of meaning', *Language*, vol. 32, pp. 195–216.

JOOS, M. (1958), 'Semology: A linguistic theory of meaning', *Studies in Linguistics*, vol. 13, pp. 53–70.

KELLY, G. (1955), *The Psychology of Personal Constructs*, vol. 1, Norton.

LOUNSBURY, F. G. (1956), 'A semantic analysis of the Pawnee kinship usage', *Language*, vol. 32, pp. 158–94.

PIKE, K. L. (1954), *Language in Relation to a Unified Theory of the Structure of Human Behavior*, part I, preliminary edn, Summer Institute of Linguistics, Glendale.

REDFIELD, R., and REDFIELD, M. P. (1940), 'Disease and its treatment in Dzitas, Yucatan', *Contributions to American Anthropology and History*, no. 32, Carnegie Institution of Washington.

SHATTUCK, G. C. (1951), *Diseases of the Tropics*, Appleton-Sentury-Crofts.

WALLACE, A., and ATKINS, J. (1960), 'The meaning of kinship terms', *American Anthropologist*, vol. 62, pp. 58–60.

WITTGENSTEIN, L. (1958), *Blue and Brown Books*, Harper & Bros.

Bibliography and Further Reading

BANKS, O. (1971), *The Sociology of Education*, Batsford.

BARATZ, S. and BARATZ, J. E., 'Early childhood intervention; the science basis of institutionalized racism', in *Language and Education*, Cashdan *et. al.*, Routledge & Kegan Paul.

BARNES, D., *et. al.* (1969), *Language, Learner and the School*, Penguin.

BECKER, H. S. (1971), 'Social class variations in the teacher–pupil relationship', reprinted in Cosin, B., *et al.* (1971).

CASTENADA, C. (1970), *The Teachings of Don Juan: A Yaqui Way of Knowledge*, Penguin.

CICOUREL, A. V., *et al.* (1973), *Language Socialization and Use in Testing and Other Educational Settings*, Seminar Press.

CICOUREL, A. V. (1973), *Cognitive Sociology*, Penguin.

CICOUREL, A. V., and KITSUSE, J. (1963), *The Educational Decision Makers*, Bobbs Merrill.

COSIN, B., *et. al.* (1971), *School and Society: A Sociological Reader*, Routledge & Kegan Paul.

COARD, B. (1971), *How the English Educational System Makes the West Indian Child Educationally Subnormal*, New Beacon Press.

DOUGLAS, J. W. B. (1964), *Home and the School*, MacGibbon & Kee.

DUMONT, R. V. and WAX, M. (1969), 'Cherokee school society and the intercultural classroom', reprinted in Cosin, B., *et al.* (1971).

FRAKE, C. (1964), 'How to ask for a drink in Subanun', reprinted in Giglioli (1972).

FRIEDMAN, N. L. (1967), 'Cultural deprivation: a commentary in the sociology of knowledge', *Journal of Educational Thought*, vol. 1, no. 1.

GAY, J., and COLE, M. (1967), *New Mathematics and an Old Culture*, Holt, Rinehart & Winston.

GEER, B., *et. al.* (1968), 'Learning the ropes', in Deutcher, I., and Thompson, E., *Among the People*, Basic Books.

GIGLIOLI, P. P. (ed.) (1972), *Language and Social Context*, Penguin.

GINSBURG, H. (1971), *The Myth of The Deprived Child*, Prentice-Hall.

GLADWIN, T. (1970), *East is a Big Bird*, Harvard University Press.

GREENE, M. (1971), 'Curriculum and consciousness', *Record*, vol. 73, no. 1, December.

HARGREAVES, D. (1967), *Social Relations in the Secondary School*, Routledge & Kegan Paul.

HORTON, R. (1967), 'African traditional thought and Western science', reprinted in Young (1971).

HORTON, R. (1968), 'Neo-Tylorianism: sound sense or sinister prejudice', *Man*, vol. 3.

KEDDIE, N. (1971), 'Classroom knowledge', in Young (1971).

OPEN UNIVERSITY CONSULTANT (1972), 'Cultural deprivation; a case in point', in *Sorting Them Out: Two essays in Social Differentiation*, Open University Press.

PLATT, A. (1968), 'The rise of the child-saving movement', reprinted in Cosin, B., *et al.* (1971).

ROSEN, H. (1972), *Language and Class*, Falling Wall Press.

TORREY, J. (1969), 'Learning to read without a teacher', *Elementary English*, April.

WAX, M., and WAX, R. (1964), *Formal Education in an American Indian Community*, Social Problems Monograph II, Spring.

WERTHMAN, C. (1971), 'Delinquents in schools', in Cosin, B., *et al.* (1971).

YOUNG, M. F. D. (1971), *Introduction to Knowledge and Control; New Directions for the Sociology of Education*, Collier Macmillan.

Acknowledgements

For permission to reproduce the Readings in this volume,
acknowledgement is made to the following:

1 Professor William Labov
2 *Harvard Educational Review*
3 *Transactions* and the author
4 *Harvard Educational Review*
5 University of Chicago Press
6 McGraw-Hill
7 American Anthropological Association